EGG PAINTING & DECORATING

305 FANTASTIC & FUN PATTERNS FOR THE WHOLE FAMILY

Pauline Pierce

Sterling Publishing Co., Inc. New York

A Sterling/Chapelle Book

For Chapelle, Ltd.

Owner: *Jo Packham*

Editor: *Malissa M. Boatwright*

Staff: *Marie Barber, Kass Burchett, Rebecca Christensen, Marilyn Goff, Michael Hannah, Shirley Heslop, Holly Hollingsworth, Susan Jorgensen, Susan Laws, Ginger Mikkelsen, Barbara Milburn, Linda Orton, Karmen Quinney, Leslie Ridenour, and Cindy Stoeckl*

Photographer: *Kevin Dilley for Hazen Photography*

Photography Styling: *Susan Laws*

Designers: *Joy Peterson-Auckner, Rebecca Carter, Holly Fuller, Kathy Griffiths, Amber Hansen, Kelly Henderson, Pauline Locke, Jamie Pierce, and Cindy Rooks*

Rebecca Carter's artwork is indicated by rooster symbol.

Library of Congress Cataloging-in-Publication Data

Pierce, pauline.
    Egg painting & decorating : 305 fantastic & fun patterns for the whole family / Pauline Pierce.
        p.   cm.
    "A Sterling/Chapelle book."
    Includes index.
    ISBN 0-8069-9895-4
    1. Egg decoration.   I. Title.
TT896.7.P54 1997
745.594'4--dc21   97-15267
                                                            CIP

10 9 8 7 6 5 4 3 2 1

Published by Sterling Publishing Company, Inc.
387 Park Avenue South, New York, N.Y. 10016
©1997 by Chapelle, Ltd.
Distributed in Canada by Sterling Publishing
c/o Canadian Manda Group, One Atlantic Avenue, Suite 105
Toronto, Ontario, Canada M6K 3E7
Distributed in Great Britain and Europe by Cassell PLC
Wellington House, 125 Strand, London WC2R OBB, England
Distributed in Australia by Capricorn Link (Australia) Pty Ltd.
P.O. Box 6651, Baulkham Hills, Business Centre, NSE 2153, Australia
Printed and Bound in China
All rights reserved

Sterling ISBN 0-8069-9895-4

A Special Thank You to:
Aleene's Paint, Delta Paint, Offray Ribbon, Plaid Paint, and Wild Fibers for graciously providing their products for projects in this book.

If you have any questions or comments or would like information on specialty products featured in this book, please contact:
Chapelle, Ltd. • P.O. Box 9252 • Ogden, UT 84409 • (801) 621-2777 • Fax (801) 621-2788

Table of Contents

Table of Contents

The Basics Before Beginning

Read The Basics Before Beginning and General Instructions before beginning project of choice to become familiar with terms and techniques used in this book.

The Egg

Because of the varying sizes of eggs, the patterns can easily be adapted to fit any size egg by reducing or enlarging as needed. Artificial eggs used in this book include: papier mâché, plastic, porcelain, styrofoam, and wooden eggs. Sizes include ⅞" to 4½".

Real eggs used in this book include: blown, hard-boiled, and ostrich eggs. Blown eggs can last from year to year, although they are more fragile than hard-boiled eggs.

Techniques used on artificial eggs are versatile and can be used on real eggs as long as all materials used are non-toxic. Note: Any real egg that is dyed can be painted with non-toxic acrylic paint.

Acrylic Gesso

A paint sealer, acrylic gesso, should be used on entire artificial egg surface before applying acrylic paint. Acrylic gesso will help prevent acrylic paint from chipping off and will help paint adhere to painting surface. Use acrylic gesso as it comes from the jar.

Baking Clay

Baking clay (polymer sculpting/modeling compound) has excellent handling qualities. It is soft and pliable, and can be baked in a home oven. It takes tooling (drilling, sanding, and painting) well and can be rolled and cut.

Baking clay is available in a variety of colors or white clay may be used, then painted.

Craft Foam

Craft foam is available in many different colors and is a great medium for embellishing eggs. It can easily be cut into any shape with everyday scissors and glued to eggs. Craft foam can be highlighted with acrylic paints.

Dyes

Commercially prepared dyes (Easter egg dye), food coloring, icing gel/concentrated paste, and corn syrup have been used on projects in this book for dying real eggs (blown or hard-boiled). Read and follow manufacturer's instructions.

Glue For Artificial Eggs

•Craft Glue

This glue is thick and all-purpose. Craft glue holds lightweight objects in place until dry, is water-soluble, flexible, and dries quickly and clear. Craft glue works well on smooth wood surfaces. Allow glue to dry thoroughly.

•Hot Glue Gun and Glue Sticks

This glue dries quickly and is available in clear, cloudy, glitter, and wood glue sticks. When used in guns, the glue is *very hot*. Use tweezers or needlenose pliers to hold small objects in place. For larger objects, use a craft stick or pencil to apply pressure until glue is hard. Strings of glue will be present, but they can be easily removed when hard. If small children are using glue guns, it is recommended that low temp glue guns be used.

•Spray Adhesive

This glue covers large surfaces. Use spray adhesive for mounting objects and covering surfaces with fabric, flowers, or paper. Spray adhesive is flammable and toxic. Use only in well-ventilated area. Read manufacturer's instructions.

•Super Glue

This glue is fast bonding, clear, and strong. Super glue is toxic and bonds everything, including fingers. Can be removed with nail polish remover (acetone). Use sparingly.

•Wood Glue, Paintable

This glue is strong, fast drying, heat-and-water resistant, safe and non-toxic. Pieces should fit snugly and a clamp should be used for best results. Allow glue to dry thoroughly.

Glue For Real Eggs

Corn syrup or a paste mixture of flour and water can be used as non-toxic glue for real eggs.

Paint

Non-toxic acrylic paints have been used on edible and non-edible projects in this book.

Acrylic paint cleans up with soap and water when wet, but it is always a good idea to use a drop cloth or something to protect work surfaces. Acrylic paint will wipe right off a non-porous surface, like tile or linoleum, or will even peel off when dry. Acrylic paint on carpet or clothes will soak in immediately and may not come completely clean.

Always allow acrylic paints to dry thoroughly before applying additional coats or colors. When a quicker drying time is necessary, a blow dryer can be used to aid in drying the paint.

If mixing colors is necessary to get a perfect shade, mix sufficient amounts to complete the project. Excess paint can be stored in airtight containers.

Paintbrushes

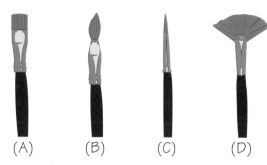

(A)   (B)   (C)   (D)

Paintbrushes are the most common tool used for painting. Good quality synthetic brushes work best when using acrylic paints. Paintbrushes come in a variety of different sizes. The size of the brush will depend on the size of pattern being painting. Small, liner brushes are used for detailing.

Every paintbrush has its own special purpose in painting. Knowing which brush to use makes painting easy.

Brushes are numbered. This refers to the shape of the metal part of brush that holds the bristles onto the shaft. The higher the number, the larger the brush. A size 10, for example, will be about an inch across. A size 5 will be about a half inch across. A size 0 or 00 is very small and is used for outline work and details.

Be certain to clean brushes thoroughly with soap and water until the water runs clean. Leaving brushes standing in water overnight will soften glue that holds the bristles and bend them out of shape.

Types of paintbrushes used for projects in this book include: flat, round, liner, and fan brushes.

•Flat

Brush (A) is a flat brush. The flat brush has long hairs and a chiseled edge for stroke work, filling in, blending, and wide sweeping strokes. Sometimes this chisel edge is used to make fine lines. More often, the flat brush is used for basecoating. Use the largest flat brush that can be handled in any given area. In this way the area can be filled in with as few strokes as

possible. The flat brush is also used in float painting technique. This is done easily because the bristles are long, have a wide chisel edge, and carry a lot of paint.

•Round

Brush (B) is a round brush. There are two types of specialty round brushes that are used for these projects — liner and round basecoater. Small round brushes have a fine point for delicate lines and detail work. They serve an entirely different purpose from flat brushes in painting. A small round brush can get into tiny areas that would be difficult to paint with a flat brush. Larger round brushes can be used to help cover large areas quickly and easily. They are very good for basecoating.

•Liner

Brush (C) is a liner brush. The liner brush is a fine-point, round brush. It is great for delicate lines, detail work, lettering, long continuous strokes, or basecoating in very small areas. Tiny dots are also done with the small round liner brush.

•Fan

Brush (D) is a fan brush. The fan brush is used to make textured looking areas, such as hair or wood grain.

Rubber Stamping & Embossing

Rubber stamps come in many shapes and sizes and are usually mounted on wood, foam, or rollers.

There are two types of ink to use with rubber stamping: pigment ink and dye-based ink.

Pigment ink pads have an ingredient that makes the ink dry slowly. The slow-drying inks allow time to add embossing powders that need to be heat-set. Pigment ink can be used without powders only on porous paper. If used on glossy paper without powder, pigment ink will never dry. Pigment pads come in many colors and are also available in white or clear.

Dye-based ink comes in one-color basic stamp pads with felt surfaces. The ink is water-soluble and quick-drying. The ink should be spread onto a clean foam pad before it is used.

Embossing powders are available in many colors. These powders are sprinkled over wet pigment inks. The excess should be shaken off, and the powder set using a heat gun.

Heat guns are made for embossing. They get very hot, but do not blow much air. They are available wherever embossing powders are sold.

Safety

Be certain to read and follow manufacturer's recommendations for materials and supplies.

It is impossible to list every safety "Do and Don't" rule, however, the following are some general safety considerations:

Clamp wood before drilling. Frequently check clamp tightness. Use safety glasses when using any power tool.

When decorating real eggs (hard-boiled or non-blown), inspect eggs before purchasing, making certain they are not dirty or cracked. Do not decorate cracked eggs as dangerous bacteria may be present. Refrigerate eggs immediately after decorating.

Sandpaper

Wooden eggs and/or surfaces that will be painted usually need to be sanded.

Sandpaper comes in many grades. Use coarse paper for rough shaping, medium for moderate sanding and fine for finish sanding. Follow manufacturer's instructions.

Sponges

Sponges are used for sponge painting. They are found in many different sizes and textures. Be certain to clean sponges thoroughly after use with soap and water until the water runs clean.

Tracing & Graphite Paper

Tracing paper is thin enough to see through and allows original pattern lines to be retraced easily.

Graphite paper is coated on one side. When it is pressed by a pencil, it transfers the graphite or chalk to the surface under it.

General Instructions For Egg Painting

Preparing Artificial Eggs

Project instructions include papier mâché, plastic, porcelain, styrofoam, and wooden eggs. Follow General Instructions For Egg Painting as follows: Sanding (wooden egg), Sealing Egg Surface (papier mâché and wooden egg), Painting Artificial Eggs, Basecoating Background (any egg), and Transferring Pattern if desired. Continue General Instructions Painting Techniques, on pages 8-9. Specific painting techniques are highlighted in project instructions.

Sanding

Read manufacturer's recommended procedures.

Sand wood in direction of the grain to create a smooth painting surface.

If project requires rounding off flat bottom, sand before painting the egg.

Check to be certain all surfaces and edges are smooth to the touch. Remove residue by wiping surfaces with a soft tacky or damp cloth.

Some projects will require the egg to be sanded to give the artwork a worn appearance. This should be done after the egg is painted and thoroughly dry and before applying spray sealer.

Sealing Egg Surface

Materials and supplies needed include acrylic gesso and large paintbrush.

Apply gesso directly to clean, unsealed surface of wooden and papier mâché egg. Note: when gesso is thinned with water it tends to cause cracking and poor adhesion.

Painting Artificial Eggs

Basecoating Background

In most cases, the project requires the entire egg surface to be painted. The number of coats needed will be determined primarily on the basecoat color being used as well as the brand of paint being used.

Materials and supplies needed include acrylic paint and large paintbrush.

Apply acrylic paint to all surfaces for full coverage. Cover the area with two to three smooth, even coats of paint. It is better to apply several thin coats of paint, rather than one heavy coat.

Transferring Pattern

If directions indicate enlarging pattern, place pattern in a photocopy machine. Set the machine to percentage required and enlarge.

Two methods of transferring pattern are given below. Choose method that is most comfortable and convenient.

Materials and supplies needed include graphite paper, manila folder or mylar, pencil, photocopy machine, scissors, tape, and tracing paper.

•Method One
The photocopy of a pattern can be traced onto tracing paper and transferred onto the egg using graphite paper.

Position carefully and tape graphite paper between pattern and egg with graphite shiny side facing egg. Firmly, trace the pattern using a pencil. Lift corner slightly and make certain the pattern is transferring.

•Method Two

The photocopy of a pattern can be traced onto and cut from a manila envelope or mylar.

Position carefully and tape cut-out pattern on egg. Carefully trace around pattern using a pencil, or if necessary, a ballpoint pen.

Remove the pattern once the design has been transferred.

Painting Techniques

Painting techniques used on projects in this book are as follows:

•Antiquing

Read manufacturer's instructions. Apply antique medium by rubbing it over wood surfaces with a clean cloth or paintbrush, wiping off any excess. Allow the antique medium to dry thoroughly. Antique medium gives an old-fashioned, aged look to new paint.

•Comma Stroke

Comma strokes are done by using a round brush. Create a dot, rotate, and decrease pressure to create the tail of a comma or tear.

•Crackle

Read manufacturer's instructions. Apply basecoat using a flat or round brush. Allow basecoat to dry thoroughly. Using an old flat or round brush, apply one coat of crackle medium using long sweeping strokes; thin coat for small cracks, thick coat for large cracks. Allow crackle medium to dry thoroughly. Apply a topcoat of contrasting color acrylic paint using a flat or round brush or a sponge. *Note: Topcoat must be applied for cracking to occur.*

•Découpage

Combine one-part water and one-part craft glue, or use ready-made découpage glue. Using an old paintbrush, paint back of artwork with glue. Place artwork piece to be découpaged; press down with fingertips to remove any air bubbles. Brush several light coats of glue over artwork. Let dry between coats. Apply several thin coats of sealer to protect it from water or weather.

•Detail

Detail painting is done after patterns have been transferred by filling in pattern with color using fine liner brush or small flat brush. It should be like coloring in a coloring book — just stay within the lines.

•Dots

Dots are made with a round object (end of paintbrush, stylus, corsage pin, or similar round tool). Load tool with paint, then dot on project until dots become smaller and smaller. Small dots are created by using a liner brush and rolling it to a point. Clean and reload dotter between dots to assure dots remain round and uniform.

•Dry-brush

Dry-brushing is done with an old flat brush dipped in a small amount of acrylic paint. Remove excess paint from brush by working in criss-cross motion on paper towel. Using the same motion, brush project with little or no pressure to create a soft texture.

•Float

Floating, to highlight and shade, is done by dipping a flat brush in water and removing excess water from brush by blotting on a paper towel. Apply acrylic paint to one side of paintbrush, brush back and forth staying in one track, until the paint fades evenly across the paintbrush. The paint will fade from dark to light.

•Marbleize

Basecoat by loading flat or round brush with three to four different colors, blending slightly. To marbleize, dip damp paintbrush into one-part water and one-part paint. Pick a point on edge of project and lay brush down. Pull brush along surface with a twisting, turning motion, making a vein. The twisting motion varies the thickness, and the turning makes a crooked, natural looking line. Some parts of the vein should have more paint than others. Veins in marble are much like the branches of a tree — irregular, splitting, and often forming a Y-shape. Repeat using a small, round liner paintbrush to make smaller veins.

•Outline

Outlining is done after patterns have been traced, transferred, and filled in with color. Paint fine outline lines, retracing if necessary. **Note: When using a rapidoliner permanent marker to outline, lightly apply spray sealer before outlining, then apply several light coats of spray sealer after outlining.** Painters with a great deal of experience may detail using a fine liner brush. Painters with little or no experience may use a .25mm tip rapidoliner permanent marker.

When using a liner brush, load paint thinned with water. Pull the brush through the paint, turning to get a fine point. Hold the brush perpendicular to the work and line the desired areas. The thickness of the line will be determined by the amount of pressure applied to the brush.

•Rubber Stamp

Cover entire rubber stamp with ink. Press stamp on desired area. Sprinkle embossing powder over stamped area. Remove excess embossing powder. If embossing powder is used, heat with embossing heat gun.

•Splatter

Splatter painting is done by applying speckles to the surface of egg. Use an old toothbrush or similar stiff bristled brush. Thin the paint with water. Dip toothbrush bristles into paint, and run finger over the bristles to splatter-paint project. The thinner the paint the larger the speckles. For very fine speckles, do not thin paint.

•Sponge

Sponge painting is done by loading the top of a sponge with paint. Blot the sponge on paper towel until most of paint has been removed. Apply the paint to the egg by lightly "blotting" the sponge up and down. Work in a circular motion starting at center of project. Some projects have called for plastic wrap instead of a sponge. Simply crinkle plastic wrap into a ball, then lightly dip into paint and sponge onto egg.

•Stencil

This technique is used to force paint through a precut surface. Hold or tape the stencil securely to the project. Load a stencil or round brush with a small amount of acrylic paint. Wipe brush on a paper towel to remove excess paint. Stipple paint into the open areas of stencil. Too much paint on the brush will cause paint to seep under the stencil. It is better to use less paint and apply several coats.

•Stipple

Stipple painting is repeated small touches using an old brush or cosmetic sponge. Load a brush or sponge with very little paint. Bounce brush tip on paper towel, then apply lightly to project. Vary dot sizes and density to create shadow or texture effect.

•Swirl

Place small amount of each paint on aluminum foil. Dip flat or round brush in each color. Swirl slightly on egg with brush, building up paint to add texture. Do not swirl too much or colors will mix together, forming a gray/brown color. Let paint dry thoroughly.

•Wash

Washing technique refers to the application of acrylic paint to a surface for transparent coverage. Mix one-part paint and three-parts water. Apply this paint wash to sealed wood using an old flat brush. Several coats of light wash produce a soft, but deep, transparent color. Allow wash to dry thoroughly between coats.

•Watercolor (Using Acrylic Paint)

(A) (B) (C) (D)

Basecoat background and transfer pattern following Basecoating Background and Transferring Pattern in General Instructions on pages 7-8. See (A).

Dilute required acrylic paint to watercolor/ink consistency with water. Refer to pattern for paint colors. Detail egg referring to pattern. See (B).

Shade egg by dipping brush in water then removing excess water from brush by blotting on a paper towel. Apply slightly darker color acrylic paint to side of brush and blend, staying on track until paint fades evenly across brush. The paint will fade from dark to light. See (C). Use a fine-tip round brush. Gently blend paint to soften edges. More water may be used if necessary to soften edges. Lightly apply stain to egg if required, then lightly apply acrylic spray sealer to artwork.

Outline pattern following Outline in General Instructions on pages 8-9 using a .25mm tip rapidoliner permanent black pen or liner brush using black paint. See (D). Apply several light coats of acrylic spray sealer to artwork.

Preparing Real Eggs

Materials needed include raw eggs, darning needle, pan, water, and vinegar.

Blown Eggs

For blown eggs, poke a hole at each end of egg with darning needle. Twist needle around inside egg to break yolk. Blow hard through hole at top of egg. Collect contents in a dish. Rinse out the egg shell and let air-dry thoroughly before decorating.

Hard-boiled Eggs

Bring eggs to room temperature. Place eggs in pan adding room temperature water to cover at least one inch above eggs. Add a teaspoon of vinegar. Slowly bring to a boil to prevent cracking. Let eggs simmer 10-15 minutes. Turn off heat and remove pan from burner. Immediately run cold water over eggs or place them in ice water until completely cooled. Dry and refrigerate, or decorate eggs immediately. Do not decorate cracked eggs.

Painting Real Eggs

Materials needed include drying container, dye solution of choice, eggs (blown or hard-boiled), egg wand, pan and water, paper towels, vegetable oil (optional), and vinegar.

Some real egg projects follow General Instructions Painting Artificial Eggs on pages 7-9: Basecoating Background, Transferring Pattern, and Painting Techniques. Specific painting techniques (Painting Artificial Eggs, Painting Real Eggs, and Dye Techniques) are highlighted in project instructions. *Note: Any real egg can be painted with non-toxic acrylic paint.*

Helpful Hints: For brighter color, leave egg in dye solution longer. Dyes will have different and unusual effects on real eggs if left submerged in solution longer than 30 minutes. For a shinier egg, apply a light coat of vegetable oil with a paper towel to dry colored egg. Dye solution can be stored in air-tight container for later use.

Dye Techniques

•Easter Egg Dye

Use cooled, hard-boiled eggs. Follow manufacturer's instructions for mixing color tablets/crystals. Dip hard-boiled egg in solution until desired shade is obtained.

•Food Colors and Egg Dye

Follow manufacturer's instructions for mixing food colors. Dip hard-boiled egg in solution until desired shade is obtained.

•Icing Gel/Concentrated Paste

Add one teaspoon vinegar, desired amount of icing gel/concentrated paste to obtain desired shade of dye solution, to ½ cup boiling water. Completely submerge eggs in solution, 5 minutes for lighter shade to 30 minutes for darker shade. Remove eggs using egg wand and set in drying container. Rinse eggs with water if a "felty" film from dye covers egg.

•Resist

Use adhesive required in project instructions (rubber cement, masking tape, or similar adhesive). Apply adhesive to egg forming a pattern as indicated in project instructions. Dip egg into darker dye solution until desired shade is obtained. Remove egg from solution and place in drying container. Let egg dry, then gently remove adhesive.

To add additional patterns, apply adhesive to colored egg forming another pattern. Dip egg into second lighter shade of dye solution until desired shade is obtained. Remove egg from solution and place in drying container. Let egg dry, then gently remove adhesive.

To color pattern left by adhesive, dip egg into second lighter shade of dye solution until desired shade is obtained. Remove egg from solution and place in drying container. Let egg dry, then gently remove adhesive.

Sculpting Baking Clay

Materials needed include acrylic gesso, acrylic paint, aluminum foil, baking clay, glue of choice, knife, oven to bake clay, paintbrush, plastic wrap, and toothpick or wire.

Place aluminum foil or plastic wrap on top of egg.

Knead clay until soft and smooth. Mold and sculpt clay into required form.

Use paintbrush end, toothpick, or wire, and knife to assist in making indentations, score lines, paint lines and, if needed, to help support clay during sculpting.

Remove desired clay form from egg. Bake clay form, following manufacturer's instructions.

Apply gesso to baked clay form.

Paint and attach pieces according to project instructions.

Sealing Paint and Artwork

The final step for artificial egg painting is applying an acrylic spray sealer to set paint and protect artwork.

Either matte sealer, for flat finish; satin sealer, for semi-gloss finish; or clear sealer, for gloss finish can be used depending on the look that is desired.

Apply several light coats to egg, not one heavy coat. Allow spray sealer to dry thoroughly.

Dyed
Eggs
44

Natural Color
Eggs
42

Metallic Ribbon
Eggs
45

Personalized
Eggs
44

Silk Organza
Eggs
45

Crepe Paper
Roll Eggs
42

Floss Wrapped
Eggs
42

Rubber Stamp
Eggs
45

Bird
Eggs
44

Dyed Plaid
Eggs
42

Valentine
Eggs
44

Total Ribbon
Wrap Eggs
43

Dotted Ribbon
Eggs
42

Plastic
Eggs
43

Green
Eggs
43

Victorian Sticker
Eggs
45

Decorative Sticker
Eggs
43

Brightly Dotted
Eggs
43

Crepe Paper
Dyed Eggs
43

Netting
Eggs
45

Monochrome
Eggs
44

Dyed Brown
Eggs
44

Dyed
Eggs
44

| Corn Syrup Striped Egg 46 | Corn Syrup & Sugar Egg 46 | Alphabet Sticker Egg 46 | Bunny Wagon Eggs 47 |

E-A-S-T-E-R
Eggs
46

Egg in Disguise	Butterfly Egg	Flying Pig Egg
47	48	50

Sunflower Egg	Button Leg Chick Egg	Bow Egg	Large Flowerpot Egg
49	49	48	48

Lamb Egg	Crow Egg Trio	Rabbit Egg	Rooster Egg	Kittens & Mittens Egg Trio	Hatched Egg
51	51	50	52	52	51

Snow Bunny
Egg
54

Angel on a Cloud
Egg
53

Rabbits in a
Shoe Eggs
53

An Eggsquisite Variety

Pink Ribbon
Egg
56

Porcelain Rose
Egg
55

Organza Ribbon
Egg
55

White Crackle
Egg
54

Ribbon
Egg
54

Gold Net
Egg
55

Plaid Egg
Trio
57

Black Button
Egg
56

Brick Finial
Egg
56

Brick
Egg
57

Sewing
Egg
57

Wax
Egg
57

Melon Egg Trio	Cock-A-Doodle Egg	Dot Eggs	Stenciled Name Egg	Cow Egg	Button Egg
58	58	56	59	59	59

Ladybug
Egg
58

Carrot
Egg Trio
60

Crow
Birdhouse Egg
60

Stenciled
Tree Egg
60

Pumpkin
Sunflower Egg
61

Candy Hearts Egg	Rosebuds Egg	Dove Egg	Birthday Present Egg	Cupcake Egg	Painted Flowers Egg	Stamped Eggs	Bird & Heart Egg	Noah's Ark Egg
61	61	63	61	62	62	62	62	63

Log Cabin	Country Home	Igloo	Thatch Cottage
Egg	Egg	Egg	Egg
63	63	64	64

Birdhouse	Flowerpot
Egg	Eggs
65	64

| Piece of Cake Egg 65 | Rose Birdhouse Egg 65 | Watering Can Egg 66 |

| Flower Button Egg 66 | Star & Fish Egg 66 | I Love You Egg 67 | Cat & Moon Egg 67 | Watermelon Egg 67 |

Eggciting For Christmas

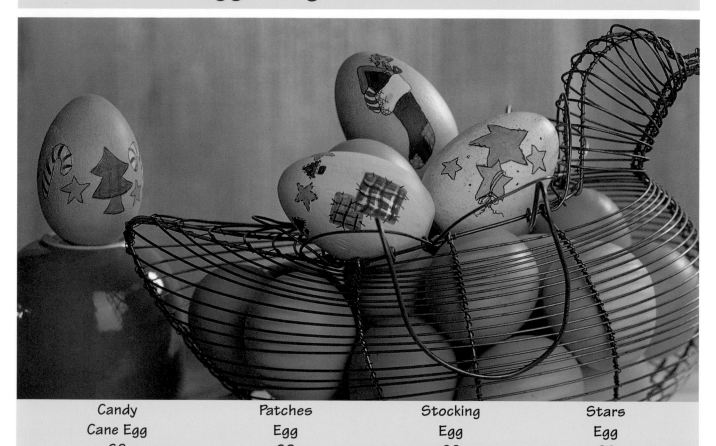

| Candy Cane Egg 68 | Patches Egg 68 | Stocking Egg 68 | Stars Egg 69 |

| Bunny in a Pocket Egg 69 | Frosty the Snowman Egg 69 | Heart & Star Egg 70 | Snowflake Snowman Egg 70 | Christmas Tree Egg 70 |

Teddy Bear Egg	Paper Reindeer Egg	Tissue Paper Tree Egg	Father Christmas Egg	Stacked Tree Eggs
71	72	71	71	72

Ornament Egg Trio	Acorn Egg	Turkey Egg	Cheese Eggs	Plum Pudding Egg	Rudolph Egg
73	73	73	74	74	74

Scarf
Snowman Egg
75

Sponged
Tree Eggs
75

Santa &
Holly Egg
72

Snow Angel
Egg
76

Christmas
Scene Egg
75

Wire Angel
Egg
76

Mosaic Seashell Egg	Potpourri Covered Egg	Winter Wonderland Egg	Frosting Egg
77	76	77	78

An Eggceptional Halloween

Spider Egg	Bat Egg	Dracula Egg	Pumpkin Egg	Trick or Treat Egg
80	79	80	80	81

Owl Egg	Chick-in Egg	Duck Egg	Stacked Pumpkin Eggs	Wire Crow Egg
81	82	82	81	82

Ghost	Witch	Frankenstein	Mummy
Egg	Egg	Egg	Egg
78	79	78	79

Dragon
Eggs
86-87

Gargoyle
Eggs
88

Whale	Penguin	Panda	Polar Bear
Egg	Eggs	Egg	Egg
83	84	84	83

Spaceship
Egg
85

Airplane
Egg
85

Spaceman
Egg
84

Ostrich Celestial
Egg
87

Ostrich Lace
Egg
88

Eggstra Easy Easter

Natural Color Eggs

Pictured on page 12

Materials:
Acrylic paint: natural colors (5); off-white. Eggs: hard-boiled (5). Paintbrush. Sponge.

Painting:
Refer to General Instructions for Painting Techniques and Preparing Real Eggs on pages 8-10. **Sponge** eggs using each color of paint for basecoat. **Wash** eggs using off-white paint.

Crepe Paper Roll Eggs

Pictured on page 13

Materials:
Crepe paper (5). Eggs: hard-boiled (5). Ribbon: wire-edged, coordinating. Scissors: craft.

Embellishing:
Refer to General Instructions for Preparing Real Eggs on pages 9-10. Using craft scissors, cut 11" circle and 11" square from crepe paper for each egg. Place egg in center of circle and square. Pull paper around egg. Tie coordinating ribbon into a bow around top of egg with circle and around both ends of egg with square.

Floss Wrapped Eggs

Pictured on page 13

Materials:
Acrylic paint: desired colors (5). Charms (5). Eggs: hard-boiled (5). Floss: overdyed, coordinating (1 skein). Glue: craft. Paintbrush. Tape: double-sided.

Painting:
Refer to General Instructions for Painting Techniques and Preparing Real Eggs on pages 8-10. **Basecoat** eggs using each color of paint.

Embellishing:
Wrap double-sided tape around middle of egg. Wrap floss around tape, ending with cross-over in front. Glue floss ends to back of egg. Glue charm in middle of cross-over.

Dyed Plaid Eggs

Pictured on page 15

Materials:
Bowls (3). Drying container. Easter egg dye: desired colors (3). Eggs: hard-boiled (3). Tape: masking.

Painting:
Refer to General Instructions for Preparing Real Eggs and Dye Techniques on pages 9-10. Using **resist** technique, wrap masking tape vertically around eggs, making certain edges of tape are flat. Add additional pattern by wrapping tape horizontally around eggs, making certain edges of tape are flat.

Dotted Ribbon Eggs

Pictured on page 16

Materials:
Acrylic paint: desired colors (3). Eggs: hard-boiled (3). Glue: hot glue gun and glue sticks. Paintbrush. Ribbon: 1¼"-wide wire-edged, coordinating, 1 yd each egg.

Painting:
Refer to General Instructions for Painting Techniques and Preparing Real Eggs on pages 8-10. **Basecoat** eggs using each color of paint.

Embellishing:
Lay ribbon flat. Place dot of hot glue in center of ribbon. Wrap ribbon vertically around eggs, narrow end of egg up. Tie bow at top of egg.

Crepe Paper Dyed Eggs

Pictured on page 17

Materials:
Bowl. Crepe paper (3). Eggs: hard-boiled (3). Rubber gloves. Water.

Embellishing:
Refer to General Instructions for Preparing Real Eggs on pages 9-10. Roll crepe paper around eggs. Wearing rubber gloves, dip eggs in bowl of water. Squeeze off excess water. Let eggs set for a few minutes. Remove crepe paper. Let eggs dry thoroughly.

Brightly Dotted Eggs

Pictured on page 17

Materials:
Acrylic paint: bright colors (5). Eggs: hard-boiled (5). Paintbrush for dots.

Painting:
Refer to General Instructions for Painting Techniques and Preparing Real Eggs on pages 8-10. **Basecoat** eggs using each color of paint. **Dot** eggs using contrasting color of paint.

Green Eggs

Pictured on page 16

Materials:
Acrylic paint: desired color. Easter egg dye: desired color. Eggs: brown, hard-boiled (3). Stickers: desired shapes. Toothbrush.

Painting:
Refer to General Instructions for Painting Techniques, Preparing Real Eggs, and Dye Techniques on pages 8-10. Attach stickers to one egg as desired for **resist** technique. Dye eggs using **Easter Egg Dye**, varying length of time eggs are submerged in dye. **Splatter** one egg using acrylic paint.

Plastic Eggs

Pictured on page 16

Materials:
Eggs: plastic (12). Fabric stitch paint: desired colors (12).

Painting:
Pull apart plastic eggs. Follow manufacturer's instructions for fabric stitch paint. Randomly add pattern onto eggs as desired. Lay egg halves on work surface to dry. Mistakes wipe right off when paint is wet. Snap egg halves together when dry.

Total Ribbon Wrap Eggs

Pictured on page 16

Materials:
Eggs: hard-boiled (4). Ribbon: 2¼"-wide, 1⅛ yds. each egg.

Embellishing:
Refer to General Instructions for Preparing Real Eggs on pages 9-10. Wrap ribbon vertically around egg with narrow end of egg down. Twist ribbon at wide end one-half turn and vertically wrap ribbon around egg, covering entire egg surface. Tie bow on top of narrow end of egg.

Decorative Sticker Eggs

Pictured on page 17

Materials:
Acrylic paint: desired colors (3). Eggs: hard-boiled (3). Paintbrush. Stickers.

Painting:
Refer to General Instructions for Painting Techniques and Preparing Real Eggs on pages 8-10. **Basecoat** eggs using each color of paint.
Embellishing:
Attach stickers to eggs as desired.

Monochrome Eggs

Pictured on page 18

Materials:
Acrylic paint: desired colors (5). Eggs: hard-boiled (5). Paintbrush. Sponges: regular; heart-shape. Toothbrush. Water.

Painting:
Refer to General Instructions for Painting Techniques and Preparing Real Eggs on pages 8-10. **Basecoat** eggs desired colors of paint going from very lt. to dk. color. Egg one, with very lt. basecoat: **splatter** egg using dk. color paint diluted with water. Egg two, with lt. basecoat: using heart-shape sponge, **sponge** egg using med. color paint. **Sponge** egg and hearts sparingly using very lt. color paint. Egg three, with med. color basecoat: **sponge** egg using very lt. color paint. Egg four, with med. dk. basecoat: using heart-shape sponge, **sponge** egg using lt. color paint. Egg five, with dk. basecoat: **splatter** egg using very lt. color paint diluted with water.

Bird Eggs

Pictured on page 14

Materials:
Acrylic paint: desired colors (5); white. Eggs: hard-boiled (5). Paintbrush. Paper towels. Toothbrush. Water.

Painting:
Refer to General Instructions for Painting Techniques and Preparing Real Eggs on pages 8-10. **Basecoat** four eggs, using each color of paint mixed with white paint. **Sponge** eggs using contrasting color of paint and paper towel crinkled into a ball then lightly dipped into paint and sponged onto eggs. **Sponge** egg without basecoat using paint diluted with water then **splatter** egg using contrasting color of paint.

Valentine Eggs

Pictured on page 15

Materials:
Acrylic paint: desired colors (5). Eggs: hard-boiled (5). Food color: desired colors (5). Glue: craft. Paintbrush. Ribbon: ⅜"-wide, desired color, ½ yd. Scissors. Stickers: coordinating. Water.

Painting:
Refer to General Instructions for Painting Techniques and Preparing Real Eggs on pages 8-10. **Basecoat** eggs by dipping paintbrush into desired food color and adding small amount of water to paintbrush.

Embellishing:
Refer to picture on page 15 to embellish eggs using stickers, ribbons, and paint as desired.

Personalized Eggs

Pictured on page 12

Materials:
Acrylic paint: desired colors (3). Eggs: hard-boiled (3). Paintbrush. Stickers.

Painting:
Refer to General Instructions for Painting Techniques and Preparing Real Eggs on pages 8-10. **Basecoat** eggs using each color of paint.

Embellishing:
Attach stickers to eggs as desired.

Dyed Eggs

Pictured on page 11 and 18

Materials:
Icing gel/concentrated paste: desired colors. Eggs: hard-boiled (26). Stickers.

Painting:
Refer to General Instructions for Preparing Real Eggs and Dye Techniques on pages 9-10. Note: Eggs can be painted in shades with non-toxic acrylic paint. Refer to Dyed Brown Eggs pictured on page 18. Dye eggs using **Icing Gel/Concentrated Paste**.

Embellishing:
Attach stickers to eggs as desired.

Victorian Sticker Eggs

Pictured on page 17

Materials:
Acrylic paint: desired colors (3); metallic gold. Eggs: hard-boiled (3). Paintbrush. Paper towels. Stickers.

Painting:
Refer to General Instructions for Painting Techniques and Preparing Real Eggs on pages 8-10. **Basecoat** eggs using each color of paint.

Embellishing:
Attach stickers to eggs as desired. Using paper towel, lightly apply metallic gold paint onto eggs for antique appearance.

Netting Eggs

Pictured on page 18

Materials:
Acrylic paint: desired colors (6). Eggs: hard-boiled (6). Paintbrush. Ribbons: 3"-wide netting, coordinating colors, 2⅜ yds. each egg; ⅜"-wide organdy, contrasting colors, 12" each egg. Scissors: fabric.

Painting:
Refer to General Instructions for Painting Techniques and Preparing Real Eggs on pages 8-10. **Basecoat** eggs using each color of paint.

Embellishing:
Place egg in center of contrasting color netting. Wrap entire egg. Twist netting and tie with coordinating organdy ribbon. Trim netting and ribbon.

Rubber Stamp Eggs

Pictured on page 14

Materials:
Acrylic paint: desired colors (5). Eggs: hard-boiled (5). Embossing powder: variety of colors. Liquid applique: white. Paintbrushes. Pigment ink: pad with variety of colors. Rubber stamps. Water.

Painting:
Refer to General Instructions for Painting Techniques and Preparing Real Eggs on pages 8-10. **Basecoat** eggs using each color of paint. **Rubber stamp** eggs as desired. **Detail** eggs using desired color paint. **Watercolor** eggs using desired color paint. Liquid applique was applied to sheep. Read and follow manufacturer's instructions for more detailed rubber stamping techniques and for liquid applique instructions.

Metallic Ribbon Eggs

Pictured on page 12

Materials:
Cording: coordinating, 6" each egg. Easter egg dye: desired colors (3). Eggs: hard-boiled (3). Ribbon: coordinating, 6" each egg. Tape: double-sided.

Embellishing:
Refer to General Instructions for Preparing Real Eggs and Dye Techniques on pages 9-10. Dye eggs using **Easter Egg Dye**. Wrap tape vertically around middle of eggs. Wrap ribbon and cording around tape.

Silk Organza Eggs

Pictured on page 12

Materials:
Eggs: hard-boiled (4). Fabric: organza, coordinating, 10" square (4). Ribbon: ¾"-wide, coordinating, 18½" each egg. Scissors: fabric.

Embellishing:
Refer to General Instructions for Preparing Real Eggs on pages 9-10. Place egg in center of oganza fabric. Wrap entire egg. Twist fabric and tie with coordinating ribbon.

Corn Syrup & Sugar Egg

Pictured on page 19

Materials:
Bowl. Egg: hard-boiled. Corn syrup: light. Food color: desired color. Paintbrush. Sugar crystals.

Painting:
Refer to General Instructions for Painting Techniques and Preparing Real Eggs on pages 8-10. Combine one drop of food color with one tablespoon lt. corn syrup in bowl. **Basecoat** top of egg. Continue adding small amounts of food color and paint egg creating a shaded effect of light to dark color.
Embellishing:
Shake sugar crystals over egg, coating completely. Let dry.

Corn Syrup Striped Egg

Pictured on page 19

Materials:
Bowls (4). Egg: hard-boiled. Corn syrup: light. Food color: desired colors (4). Paintbrush. Sugar crystals.

Painting:
Refer to General Instructions for Painting Techniques and Preparing Real Eggs on pages 8-10. Combine one drop of each food color with one tablespoon lt. corn syrup in separate bowls. **Basecoat** colored stripes onto egg.
Embellishing:
Shake sugar crystals over egg coating completely. Let dry.

Alphabet Sticker Egg

Pictured on page 19

Materials:
Acrylic gesso. Acrylic paint: aqua; blue/green; med. blue; med. green; med. orange; med. pink; white; yellow. Acrylic spray sealer. Egg: wooden, 2½". Paintbrushes. Stickers: alphabet.

Painting:
Refer to General Instructions For Egg Painting on pages 7-10. Prepare egg for painting. **Detail** egg referring to pattern. Apply spray sealer.
Embellishing:
Refer to picture on page 19. Attach alphabet stickers to egg as desired.

E-A-S-T-E-R Eggs

Pictured on page 19

Materials:
Acrylic gesso. Acrylic paint: pale blue; pale blue/green; gray; gray/green; pink; purple; lt. red; white; yellow. Acrylic spray sealer. Eggs: wooden, 2½" (6). Paintbrushes.

Painting:
Refer to General Instructions For Egg Painting on pages 7-10. Prepare eggs for painting. **Basecoat** eggs using white paint. **Detail** eggs referring to patterns. Patterns repeat around eggs.

Bunny Wagon Eggs

Pictured on page 19

Materials:
Acrylic gesso. Acrylic paint: lt. blue; lt. green; med. green; peach; pink; purple; metallic pearl/white; lt. yellow. Acrylic spray sealer. Dowel: wooden, ¼" x 36". Eggs: wooden, 2½" (2); ⅞" Easter eggs (10). Flowerpots: clay, 5", for bunny wagon; 2½", for tulips; 1½", for Easter eggs. Glue: hot glue gun and glue sticks. Hammer. Hearts: wooden, ½" (4). Knife: craft. Needle: hand-sewing. Pen: fine-tip permanent, black. Paintbrushes. Pencil. Ribbons: 1¼"-wide wire-edged yellow dotted, 20"; 1¼"-wide wire-edged purple dotted, 20"; ½"-wide wire-edged pink, 12"; ½"-wide plaid, 12"; ¼"-wide green satin, 1 yd. Saw. Scissors. Sewing machine. Spanish moss. Sponge: ½" x ½". Styrofoam block: 2" x 6" x 4". Thread: coordinating. Tracing or graphite paper. Tulips: wooden, 1¾" tall with predrilled ¼" hole in bottom (3). Wheels: wooden, 1½" diameter (4).

Painting:
Refer to General Instructions For Egg Painting on pages 7-10. Refer to picture on page 19. Cut dowel into five pieces; two 4½" lengths for wagon axles and three 5" lengths for tulip stems. Prepare eggs, flowerpots, tulips, wheels, axles, tulip stems, and hearts for painting. **Basecoat** one 2½" egg using purple, one 2½" egg using lt. yellow, flowerpots using pink, one tulip using lt. yellow, one using lt. blue, one using pink, wheels using pink, axles using lt. yellow, tulip stems using lt. green, and hearts using lt. blue paint. **Sponge** over tulips, two smaller flowerpots, and wheels using metallic pearl/white paint. **Sponge** checkerboard effect around top rim of large flowerpot with metallic pearl/white, lt. blue, and med. green paint. **Detail** bunny faces using pen.

Embellishing:
Refer to Bunny Wagon Eggs Pattern on page 89. Cut out two yellow dotted and two purple dotted ribbons into 10" lengths. Transfer sewing lines. With right sides together, fold one ribbon length in half. Machine-stitch along sewing line, leaving bottom edge open to turn. Repeat for total of two yellow dotted ears and two purple dotted ears. Turn each ear right side out and whip-stitch bottom edge closed. Tie one bow from plaid and pink ribbons. Using hammer, tap wheels onto axles. Using hot glue gun and glue stick, hot-glue hearts to center of wheels. Hot-glue axles to bottom of wagon. Hot-glue ears and bows on bunnies. Hot-glue Easter eggs into small flowerpot. Using craft knife, cut styrofoam to fit wagon and medium flowerpot. Cut four 3" lengths from ¼"-wide green ribbon for tulip leaves. Hot-glue leaves onto tulip stems. Insert tulip stems into styrofoam inside medium flowerpot. Hot-glue medium and small flowerpots in back of wagon. Hot-glue bunnies in front of medium and small flowerpots. Hot-glue Spanish moss on top of medium flowerpot and wagon.

Egg in Disguise

Pictured on page 20

Materials:
Acrylic gesso. Acrylic paint: dk. flesh; dk. gray; white. Acrylic spray sealer. Cotton balls: (2). Egg: wooden, 4½". Felt squares: white; pink. Glue: hot glue gun and glue sticks. Paintbrushes. Ribbon: ¼"-wide satin, white, 24". Scissors.

Painting:
Refer to General Instructions For Egg Painting on pages 7-10. Prepare egg for painting. **Basecoat** egg using white paint. **Detail** egg referring to pattern. **Stipple** cheeks using dk. flesh paint. Apply spray sealer.

Embellishing:
Refer to Egg in Disguise Patterns on page 90 and picture on page 20. Cut out two hats, two feet, and two outer ears from white felt. Cut out two inner ears, two foot pads, and six toes from pink felt. Using hot glue gun and glue stick, hot-glue inner ears onto outer ears. Hot-glue foot pads and toes to feet. Hot-glue front of hat to head. Trim curves if necessary. Hot-glue ears to top of hat. Hot-glue back of hat to head. Hot-glue feet to front of egg. Hot-glue ribbon around edge of hat. Hot-glue two cotton balls onto egg for tail.

Butterfly Egg

Pictured on page 20

Materials:
Acrylic gesso. Acrylic paint: dk. gray; lt. pink; purple/blue; med. tan; white; off-white. Acrylic spray sealer. Awl. Egg: wooden, 2½". Embroidery floss: purple/blue, 12". Felt: pink; purple/blue; creamy yellow. Glitter glaze. Glue: craft; hot glue gun and glue sticks; wood. Paintbrushes. Pen: fine-tip permanent, black. Scissors. Wire: beading, gold, 10". Wire cutters. Wooden knob: 1", flat on one side.

Painting:
Refer to General Instructions For Egg Painting on pages 7-10. Using wood glue, attach wooden knob to egg for butterfly head. Prepare egg and head for painting. **Basecoat** egg and head using med. tan paint. **Detail** egg referring to pattern. **Outline** nose, mouth, and cheeks using pen. Apply spray sealer. Apply glitter glaze over head and body.

Embellishing:
Refer to picture on page 20. Using awl, pierce two holes in top of head for antennas. Cut two 5" lengths of wire. Fold each length of wire in half. Twist wire leaving a loop at the end. Spiral wire around end of small paintbrush. Using craft glue, glue wire into holes for antennas. Refer to Butterfly Egg Patterns on page 89. Cut out two large wings and two small wings for outer wings from creamy yellow felt. Cut additional wing pieces from pink and purple/blue felt. Refer to picture on page 20. Using hot glue gun and glue stick, hot-glue wing pieces together. Hot-glue wings to egg. Tie small bow around butterfly neck using embroidery floss.

Large Flowerpot Egg

Pictured on page 20

Materials:
Acrylic gesso. Acrylic paint: lt. blue; med. blue; lt. brown; med. brown; gold; dk. green; med. green; pale olive green; dull mauve; lt. pink; med. pink; med. purple; lt. tan; white; lt. yellow. Acrylic spray sealer. Egg: wooden, 4½". Paintbrushes. Pen: fine-tip permanent, black. Sponge. Spray stain: walnut.

Painting:
Refer to General Instructions For Egg Painting on pages 7-10. Prepare egg for painting. **Wash** in colors then **stipple** with same color, referring to pattern. **Sponge** sky lightly using white paint. Apply spray stain. **Outline** egg using pen.

Bow Egg

Pictured on page 20

Materials:
Acrylic gesso. Acrylic paint: dk. gray; med. dull pink; lt. purple; violet; white. Acrylic spray sealer. Egg: wooden, 4½". Paintbrushes. Pen: fine-tip permanent, black. Toothbrush.

Painting:
Refer to General Instructions For Egg Painting on pages 7-10. Prepare egg for painting. **Basecoat** egg using med. dull pink paint. **Detail** bow, referring to pattern. **Watercolor** vertical lines, then horizontal lines of bow using white paint. **Float** bow using dk. gray paint. **Splatter** egg using white paint. **Outline** egg using pen.

Button Leg Chick Egg

Pictured on page 20

Materials:
Acrylic gesso. Acrylic paint: black; cream; lt. blue; orange; med. pink; med. yellow; pale yellow; white. Acrylic spray sealer. Buttons: ¼"-½" two-hole, desired colors (45-50). Crackle medium. Egg: wooden, 4½". Glue: hot glue gun and glue sticks. Knife: craft. Paintbrushes. Pen: fine-tip permanent, black. Wire: fine-gauge, jewelry, 12". Wire cutters. Wood: ⅛"-thick, balsa, 7" x 7".

Painting:
Refer to General Instructions For Egg Painting on pages 7-10. Refer to Button Leg Chick Egg Patterns on page 89. Using craft knife, cut out two wings and two foot patterns from balsa wood. Prepare egg and wood for painting. **Basecoat** egg, wings, and feet using med. yellow paint. Apply **crackle** medium to egg, wings, and feet. Apply topcoat to egg, wings, and feet using pale yellow paint. Paint bottom one-third of egg using cream paint. **Detail** egg referring to pattern.

Embellishing:
Cut wire into two 6" lengths. Fold each length of wire in half. Thread buttons on wire to measure 2½" long. Twist ends of wire together. Refer to picture on page 20. Using hot glue gun and glue stick, hot-glue feet to button legs. Hot-glue legs and wings to egg. **Outline** broken eggshell design using pen.

Sunflower Egg

Pictured on page 20

Materials:
Acrylic gesso. Acrylic paint: green; pink; dk. pink; lt. pink; white; yellow. Acrylic spray sealer. Cotton swabs. Egg half: wooden, 2". Florist foam. Flowerpot: wooden, 2". Glue: hot glue gun and glue sticks. Knife: craft. Paintbrushes. Pen: fine-tip permanent, black. Pencil. Sandpaper. Spanish moss. Wood: balsa, ⅛" thick. Wire: craft, 8".

Painting:
Refer to General Instructions For Egg Painting on pages 7-10. Refer to Sunflower Egg Patterns on page 92. Using craft knife, cut out one flower and two leaves from balsa wood. Prepare egg, flowerpot, and wood pieces for painting. **Basecoat** half egg using yellow, flower using pink, leaves using green, and flowerpot using lt. pink paint. **Detail** egg and wood pieces referring to pattern. **Dot** cheeks using dk. pink paint and cotton swab. **Outline** egg, leaves, and flower using pen.

Embellishing:
Using craft knife, cut florist foam to fit flowerpot. Using hot glue gun and glue stick, hot-glue florist foam inside flowerpot. Hot-glue Spanish moss on top of florist foam. Twist wire around pencil for stem. Hot-glue half egg to flower with wire stem glued between. Hot-glue leaves to wire stem. Insert stem into pot.

Flying Pig Egg

Pictured on page 20

Materials:
Acrylic gesso. Acrylic paint: black; pink; dk. pink; white. Acrylic spray sealer. Baking clay: pink; yellow. Dowel: wooden, ½" x 12". Drill with ⅟₁₆" and ½" bits. Egg: wooden, 4½". Eye screw: small. Fishing line. Glue: craft. Paintbrushes. Sandpaper. Saw.

Painting:
Refer to General Instructions for Egg Painting and Sculpting Baking Clay on pages 7-10. Sand flat bottom of egg to round off. Drill four ½" holes for legs, referring to pattern and one ⅟₁₆" hole for eye screw on top of egg. Cut dowel into four 2" lengths and saw ¼" slots in end of feet. Sand any rough edges. Glue dowels into ½" holes. Prepare egg for painting. **Basecoat** egg and dowels using pink paint. **Detail** egg and dowels referring to pattern. **Float** across nose, around legs, knees, and bottom using dk. pink paint.

Embellishing:
Sculpt pink clay into ears and tail. Curl tail. Refer to Flying Pig Egg Diagram on page 90 for wings. Mold yellow clay into diagram shapes, flatten, and push together to make wings. Bake clay following manufacturer's instructions. Using craft glue, secure tail, ears, and wings to egg. Attach eye screw and hang with fishing line.

Rabbit Egg

Pictured on page 21

Materials:
Acrylic gesso. Acrylic paint: black; med. blue/gray; pink; white. Baking clay: orange; white. Dowel: wooden, ⅛" x 1½". Drill with ⅛" bit. Eggs: 2¾"; 1¾". Glue: craft; wood. Greenery for carrot top. Knife: craft. Paintbrushes. Ribbon: ⅜"-wide, polka dot, 12". Saw. Toothpick.

Painting:
Refer to General Instructions For Egg Painting and Sculpting Baking Clay on pages 7-10. Drill ⅛" hole in narrow end of 2¾" egg (body) and wide end of 1¾" egg (head). Cut dowel to fit between body and head. Using wood glue, secure head to body. Sculpt white clay into back legs. Form to body. Sculpt white clay into back paws. Using craft knife, cut into clay for toes. Attach back paws to back legs. Cut fur markings into clay. Sculpt white clay into ears. Form to head. Sculpt white clay into front paws. Cut into clay for toes. Attach front paws to body. Sculpt orange clay into carrot. Using toothpick, make a small hole in top of carrot for greenery. Cut markings into carrot. Bake clay, following manufacturer's instructions. Prepare egg and clay pieces for painting. **Basecoat** egg and clay pieces using white paint. **Detail** egg and clay pieces referring to pattern. Using craft glue, attach carrot between front paws. Place greenery in small hole at top of carrot. Glue clay parts to body.

Embellishing:
Tie ribbon around neck.

Hatched Egg

Pictured on page 21

Materials:
Acrylic gesso. Acrylic paint: black; med. flesh; dk. gray; lt. orange; med. orange; white; yellow; lt. yellow. Acrylic spray sealer. Down feather: white. Egg: wooden, 2½". Felt: bright yellow; lt. yellow. Glue: hot glue gun and glue sticks. Paintbrushes. Scissors.

Painting:
Refer to General Instructions For Egg Painting on pages 7-10. Prepare egg for painting. **Basecoat** egg using lt. yellow paint. **Detail** egg referring to pattern. **Float** around top and left side of beak area using med. orange paint. **Float** under cheeks and beak using yellow paint. **Wash** cheeks using med. flesh paint. **Float** top of cheeks using white paint. **Dot** eyes using black paint. Apply spray sealer.

Embellishing:
Refer to Hatched Egg Patterns on page 90 and picture on page 21. Cut two feet and two large wings from bright yellow felt. Cut two small wings from lt. yellow felt. Make small cuts in wings. Using hot glue gun and glue stick, hot-glue large wings onto each side of egg. Hot-glue small wings onto each large wing. Hot-glue feet to egg. Hot-glue feather on top of egg.

Lamb Egg

Pictured on page 21

Materials:
Acrylic gesso. Acrylic paint: black; flesh; lt. ivory; lt. mauve; white. Acrylic spray sealer. Doll hair: cotton, off-white with tight curls, 1 pkg. Eggs: wooden, 3½" for body; 1" for legs (4); Half egg: wooden for head, 1½". Felt: black, small scrap. Glue: hot glue gun and glue sticks. Paintbrushes. Scissors: craft.

Painting:
Refer to General Instructions For Egg Painting on pages 7-10. Prepare eggs for painting. **Basecoat** half egg using lt. ivory paint. **Detail** face referring to pattern. **Float** to shade around half egg using flesh paint. **Stipple** cheeks using lt. mauve paint. **Float** top of cheeks using white paint. **Basecoat** four 1" eggs using black paint for legs.

Embellishing:
Using hot glue gun and glue stick, hot-glue leg eggs, narrow end up, to 3½" egg for body. Hot-glue doll hair to body, working small areas at a time. Refer to Lamb Egg Patterns on page 90. Cut out two ears and one tail from black felt. Hot-glue tail to end of body egg. Hot-glue half egg to body egg. Hot-glue ears to half egg. Hot-glue doll hair to top of head egg. Apply spray sealer.

Crow Egg Trio

Pictured on page 21

Materials
Acrylic gesso. Acrylic paint: black; brown; med. gold; white; lt. yellow. Acrylic spray sealer. Eggs: wooden, 2½"; 2"; 1½". Glue: hot glue gun and glue sticks. Hearts: wooden 1¾"; 1⅛"; ⅞" for feet. Paintbrushes. Straw hats: varying sizes (3). Sunflower: small, silk

Painting:
Refer to General Instructions For Egg Painting on pages 7-10. Prepare eggs and hearts for painting. **Basecoat** eggs using black paint. **Detail** eggs referring to pattern. **Basecoat** hearts using med. gold paint. **Float** to highlight hearts using lt. yellow paint. **Comma stroke** and **dot** hearts using white paint.

Embellishing:
Refer to picture on page 21. Using hot glue gun and glue stick, hot-glue hearts on bottom of eggs for feet, using large heart on large egg, etc. Hot-glue hats on eggs. Hot-glue sunflower on middle-sized hat.

Kittens & Mittens Egg Trio

Pictured on page 21

Materials:
Acrylic gesso. Acrylic paint: blue/gray; lt. blue; gray; pink; white; yellow; lt. yellow. Acrylic spray sealer. Awl. Baking clay: white. Beads: ¼", frosted white (3). Eggs: wooden, 2½" (3). Eye screws: 1⁄16" (12). Fabric: pink pseudo-suede 11" x 17". Glue: hot glue gun and glue sticks. Needle: hand-sewing. Paintbrushes. Pegs: wooden, 1¼" (6). Pen: fine-tip permanent, black. Pliers. Ruler. Scissors: fabric. Thread: coordinating. Wire: thin, 6". Wire cutters.

Painting:
Refer to General Instructions For Egg Painting and Sculpting Baking Clay on pages 7-10. Sculpt clay into 6 kitten ears. Bake clay, following manufacturer's instructions. Hot-glue two ears to each egg. Prepare eggs, clay, and wooden pegs for painting. **Basecoat** one egg and two pegs using lt. yellow, one egg and two pegs using gray, and one egg and two pegs using white paint. **Detail** eggs and ears referring to pattern. **Detail** legs referring to picture on page 21. **Dot** eyes using lt. blue paint. **Outline** egg using pen.

Embellishing:
Refer to Kittens & Mittens Egg Trio Pattern on page 90. Cut out 6 hats from suede fabric. Using needle and thread, sew two hat pieces, right sides together, along one side. Gather-stitch along dotted line. Pull gathers slightly and secure thread. Turn hats right side out. Turn edges of hats under and hot-glue to top of eggs. Sew one bead to tip of each hat. Using an awl, pierce two holes in bottom of each egg ¾" apart. Pierce end of pegs and attach eye screws in bottom of each egg and in bottom of each peg. Using wire cutters, cut six 1" lengths of wire. Using pliers, thread and wrap wire around eye screws to attach legs to body. Twist ends together and cut off excess wire.

Rooster Egg

Pictured on page 21

Materials:
Acrylic gesso. Acrylic paint: black; blue; orange; white; yellow. Acrylic spray sealer. Egg: wooden, 2½". Glue: hot glue gun and glue sticks; super. Craft foam: orange; red. Feathers: small, blue; lavender; purple. Paintbrushes. Spools: 5⁄8", wooden (2).

Painting:
Refer to General Instructions For Egg Painting on pages 7-10. Prepare egg for painting. **Basecoat** egg using white paint. **Detail** egg referring to pattern. Paint spools using orange paint.

Embellishing:
Refer to Rooster Egg Patterns on page 91. Cut two feet and one upper and lower beak from orange foam. Cut two waddles and one comb from red foam. Super-glue comb to top of egg. Fold beak pieces in half and hot-glue under comb. Super-glue waddles to beak. Super-glue spools to bottom of egg. Using hot glue gun and glue stick, hot-glue feet to spools. Hot-glue feathers on egg for tail.

Rabbits in a Shoe Eggs

Pictured on page 22

Materials:

Acrylic gesso. Acrylic paint: black; dk. blue; lt. blue; dk. brown; dk. pink; lt. pink; med. pink; white; dk. yellow; lt. yellow. Acrylic spray sealer. Craft foam: white. Drill with bit width of wire. Eggs: wooden, 1½"; 1" (3). Floss: overdyed, coordinating colors (1 skein). Glue: craft. Needle: large-eyed; hand-sewing. Paintbrushes. Ribbons: ⅛"-wide, green 4"; ¾"-wide wire-edged, coordinating 6". Sandpaper. Scissors: craft. Shoe: papier mâché, 6½" long. Toothpicks. Wire: braided, 1 yd. Wire cutters.

Painting:

Refer to General Instructions For Egg Painting on pages 7-10. Prepare eggs and papier mâché shoe for painting. **Dry-brush** shoe using lt. blue over dk. blue paint for basecoat. **Detail** shoe, referring to picture on page 22. Slightly sand door and windows on shoe for worn appearance before applying spray sealer.

Embellishing:

Using floss in strands of three, thread into large-eyed needle and lace shoe. Tie floss into bow. Drill two holes in each egg for legs. Drill two holes in each egg for arms. Twist wire around toothpick to make arms. Using craft glue, secure arms into drilled holes. Twist wire around toothpick to make legs. Make loops in end of wire for feet. Glue legs into drilled holes. **Dot** eyes using black paint. **Dot** nose using black paint. Paint a straight line down from nose. Refer to Rabbits in a Shoe Eggs Patterns on page 91. Using craft scissors, cut 6 small ears and 2 large ears from craft foam. Paint middle section of ears using lt. pink paint. Glue ears on rabbits' heads. Make one small bow using ⅛" green ribbon. Glue bow between ears on largest rabbit. Sew gathering-stitch along ¾"-wide ribbon to make skirt. Pull gather and secure thread. Glue skirt around largest rabbit's waist. Twist wire to make one pair of glasses. Glue glasses on largest rabbit. Randomly glue rabbits on papier mâché shoe.

Angel on a Cloud Egg

Pictured on page 22

Materials:

Acrylic gesso. Acrylic paint: black; blue; lt. flesh; metallic gold; gray; pink; metallic silver; white. Ball: wooden, 1¼". Cardboard: 4½" square. Doll hair: cream, curly. Drill with ³⁄₁₆" bit. Egg: wooden, 2½". Glue: craft. Half eggs: wooden, ⅞" (2). Hearts: wooden, 1" (2). Paintbrushes. Pencil. Scissors. Star: wooden, 1". Wire: silver, braided.

Painting:

Refer to General Instructions For Egg Painting on pages 7-10. Drill ³⁄₁₆" hole into top and bottom of wooden ball, one end of half eggs, and heart points. Drill ³⁄₁₆" hole into bottom of star. Drill two holes in bottom of egg for legs and two holes in upper back of egg for wings. Prepare eggs, wooden ball, hearts, and star for painting. **Basecoat** 2½" egg using white, wooden ball and half eggs using flesh, hearts using metallic silver, and star using metallic gold paint. **Detail** egg and wooden ball referring to pattern. **Float** blue paint over and under sleeves on egg.

Embellishing:

Wind wire around pencil and cut two 2½"coiled lengths for legs, two 1½" coiled lengths for wings, one ½" coiled length for neck, and one 1½" coiled length for star. Using craft glue, secure one end of each 2½" length of wire into each half egg for feet and other end of wire into body. Glue one end of each 1½" length of wire into each heart for wings and other end of wire into upper back of body. Glue one end of 1½" wire into star and other end of wire into top of wooden ball. Wind hair loosely around cardboard 24 times. Slide hair off cardboard. Using one strand of hair, tie hair in middle to secure. Glue hair to top of wooden ball spreading out to cover entire head, with star in center. Glue one end of ½" of neck wire into bottom of wooden ball and other end of wire into top of egg.

Snow Bunny Egg

Pictured on page 22

Materials:
Acrylic gesso. Acrylic paint: black; white. Egg: wooden, 2". Glue: hot glue gun and glue sticks. Paintbrushes. Scissors. Sparkle glaze. Sponge. Texture medium: snow. Trim: clear opalescent garland floss, 20". Water. Wire: thin, gold, 14". Wire cutters.

Painting:
Refer to General Instructions For Egg Painting on pages 7-10. **Basecoat** egg using white paint. Dampen sponge and apply snow texture over egg using a patting motion. **Detail** egg referring to picture on page 22. Apply sparkle glaze to egg.

Embellishing:
Using wire cutters, cut two 7" lengths of wire. Cut two 8" lengths of garland floss. Using hot glue gun and glue stick, hot-glue one end of floss to one end of wire. Twist floss around wire and secure with hot glue. Repeat for other ear. Form wire into ear shapes. Hot-glue ears to top of egg. Using remaining floss, tie several loose knots to form tail. Hot-glue tail to egg.

An Eggsquisite Variety

White Crackle Egg

Pictured on page 23

Materials:
Acrylic gesso. Acrylic paint: white; med. yellow. Acrylic spray sealer. Crackle medium. Egg: wooden, 2½.". Glue: hot glue gun and glue sticks. Charms: ¾" porcelain leaf, white (2); 1" porcelain rose, white. Paintbrushes. Trim: white pearls, 8½".

Painting:
Refer to General Instructions For Egg Painting on pages 7-10. Refer to picture on page 23. Prepare egg for painting. **Basecoat** egg using med. yellow paint. Apply **crackle** medium. Apply topcoat to egg using white paint.

Embellishing:
Using hot glue gun and glue stick, hot-glue rose, leaves, and pearl trim onto egg.

Ribbon Egg

Pictured on page 23

Materials:
Batting: 4" x 4". Braid: gold, 22"; white, 11". Bead 8mm: gold. Charm: angel wing (2). Egg 2-part: porcelain unglazed, 4½". Fabric: 4" x 4" gold satin. Glitter spray: gold. Glue: hot glue gun and glue sticks. Needle: hand sewing. Ribbons: 1¼"-wide wire-edged, gold mesh, 9"; ⅞"-wide gold lamé, 5"; ⅞"-wide gold/white divine, 8"; ⅝"-wide gold/white divine, 20"; 1½"-wide white/gold, 8". Scissors: fabric. Thread: coordinating. Trim: gold metallic wire braid, 3".

Painting:
Spray egg with glitter spray.

Embellishing:
Refer to Ribbon Diagrams on page 93. Make one **Fan** using 5" length of ⅞"-wide lamé ribbon. Using hot glue gun and glue stick, hot-glue in place on top of egg. Make one **5-Petal Flower** using 8" length of 1½"-wide gold trimmed white ribbon. Hot-glue in place on top of egg. Hot-glue gold bead in center of 5-petal flower. Make one **Gathered Flower, Single-Ribbon** using 8" length of ⅞"-wide divine ribbon. Hot-glue on top of egg. Make two **Gathered Flower(s), Double-Ribbon** using four 5" lengths of ⅝"-wide divine. Hot-glue one double-ribbon gathered flower on top of egg. Set aside second double-ribbon gathered flower. Make one **Poppy** using 9" length of 1¼" gold wired mesh ribbon. Hot-glue on top of egg. Hot-glue angel wing charms together like butterfly wings. Wrap gold braid around wings to hide hot glue. Hot-glue wings to top of egg. Using open side of bottom egg, trace egg on wrong side of satin fabric and batting. Cut out fabric and batting. Hot-glue batting to inside bottom of egg. Use a gathering stitch on outside edge of satin fabric. Gather slightly to fit into bottom of egg. Hot-glue satin fabric inside egg, ½" from top of egg. Cover raw edge of satin fabric with white braid. Hot-glue braid in place. Cut gold braid into two 11" lengths. Hot-glue one around edge of top egg and one around edge of bottom egg. Hot-glue second double-ribbon gathered flower inside bottom egg.

Porcelain Rose Egg

Pictured on page 23

Materials:

Acrylic paint: lavender; lt. pink; white. Acrylic spray sealer. Cording: satin, cream, 2¼ yds. Egg: papier mâché, 5". Glue: hot glue gun and glue sticks. Paintbrushes. Pencil. Plastic wrap. Ribbon: ½"-wide sheer pink, 1 yd. Roses: ¼" porcelain, lavender (16), lt. pink (16). Tape measure.

Painting:

Refer to General Instructions For Egg Painting on pages 7-10. Refer to picture on page 23. Prepare egg for painting. **Basecoat** egg using lavender paint, and plastic wrap crinkled into a ball. **Sponge** sparingly using lt. pink then white paint.

Embellishing:

Starting at top of narrow end of egg, measure down 5½". Using pencil, mark a circle around egg. Using hot glue gun and glue stick, hot-glue four lt. pink porcelain roses, evenly spaced, around 5½" mark. Measure down 3½", 2", then 1" and repeat above process alternating rose colors to complete egg. Hot-glue end of cording to top of egg. Wind cording down and around lt. pink rose at 5½" mark, then back up to top of egg. Hot-glue cording to secure. Wind cording down opposite side of egg in same manner. Repeat until all roses have cording going around them. Wrap and hot-glue cording around top of egg. Tie bow using pink ribbon. Hot-glue on top of cording for hanger.

Organza Ribbon Egg

Pictured on page 23

Materials:

Acrylic gesso. Acrylic paint: pink. Acrylic spray sealer. Egg: wooden, 4½". Glue: hot glue gun and glue sticks. Paintbrush. Ribbons: 3"-wide sheer organza, green, yellow, blue, 3 yds. each; ½"-wide pink, ½ yd. Rubber band. Scissors: fabric. Tape measure.

Painting:

Refer to General Instructions For Egg Painting on pages 7-10. Prepare egg for painting. **Basecoat** egg using pink paint.

Embellishing:

Refer to picture on page 23. Using fabric scissors, cut 3"-wide ribbon into six 36" lengths. Using hot glue gun and glue stick, center and hot-glue one length of ribbon on bottom of egg. Bring ribbon to top along both sides of egg. Repeat with each ribbon gluing in a spoke-like manner to bottom of egg. Secure ribbons on top with rubber band. Fold ribbon ends over and secure under rubber band. Use remaining 3" pieces to weave around egg through the vertical ribbons, starting with blue, then yellow, green, and blue until entire egg is covered. Using ½"-wide ribbon, tie a multi-loop bow. Tuck ends of ribbon into rubber band.

Gold Net Egg

Pictured on page 23

Materials:

Egg 2-part: porcelain unglazed, 4¼". Glue: hot glue gun and glue sticks. Pens: med.-tip permanent, metallic gold; calligraphy, gold. Pencil. Ribbons: 3⅛"-wide gold metallic elan, 7"; ⅞"-wide sheer metallic stripe, 7". Scissors: fabric. Trim: metallic gold rose.

Embellishing:

Refer to picture on page 23. Stretch elan over top of egg. Turn under edge to rim, cutting away excess. Using hot glue gun and glue stick, hot-glue to secure ribbon (spread glue thinly to avoid build up). Hot-glue one end of sheer ribbon under edge to rim at center back. Pull over top lengthwise and secure at center front of egg with hot glue. Hot-glue rose on top of egg, centering on ribbon. On bottom egg, pencil in words such as Joy, Hope, Love, alternating angle of each word. Using calligraphy pen, outline lettering (keep pen tip flat). Let egg dry between words. Using metallic gold pen, draw a gold line around upper and lower edges of bottom half of egg.

Pink Ribbon Egg

Pictured on page 23

Materials:

Acrylic gesso. Acrylic paint: pink. Acrylic spray sealer. Egg: wooden, 4½". Paintbrush. Ribbon: 1½"-wide wire-edged pink/white ombre, ½ yd. Scissors.

Painting:

Refer to General Instructions For Egg Painting on pages 7-10. Prepare egg for painting. **Basecoat** egg using pink paint. Apply spray sealer.

Embellishing:

Refer to picture on page 23. Wrap ribbon around egg and tie in bow on top of egg.

Black Button Egg

Pictured on page 24

Materials:

Acrylic gesso. Acrylic paint: dk. brown; med. brown; metallic copper; metallic gold; very pale yellow. Acrylic spray sealer. Buttons: black; gold. Drill with ⅜6" bit. Egg: wooden, 2½". Glue: craft. Napkin ring: decorative for holder. Paintbrushes. Sponge. Wire: florist, 1". Wire cutters.

Painting:

Refer to General Instructions For Egg Painting on pages 7-10. Prepare egg for painting. Refer to picture on page 24. **Sponge** egg using dk. brown paint for basecoat. **Sponge** egg lightly using med. brown, then very pale yellow paint. **Marbleize** egg using metallic gold and metallic copper paint.

Embellishing:

Drill ⅜6" hole in top end of egg. Using craft glue, insert and glue into drilled hole. Wrap wire onto black button and glue to secure. Using wire cutters, cut back of gold button off and glue gold button on top of black button. Place on napkin ring for holder.

Brick Finial Egg

Pictured on page 24

Materials:

Acrylic gesso. Acrylic paint: black; dk. brown; med. brown; clay; flesh; metallic gold; ivory; med. tan. Acrylic spray sealer. Candle cup: wooden, 1½". Candlestick holder: wooden, 2". Doll pin stand: 1". Egg: wooden, 2½". Glue: wood. Miniature bricks: ⅜" square (9). Paintbrushes. Rubber stamp: ⅜" square. Toothbrush.

Painting:

Refer to General Instructions For Egg Painting on pages 7-10. Refer to picture on page 24. Prepare egg for painting. **Sponge** egg sparingly using clay paint for basecoat. **Sponge** egg using flesh, then ivory paint. **Splatter** egg using dk. brown paint. **Stamp** brick squares randomly onto egg using black and clay paint. Paint candle cup and doll pin stand using black paint. Paint ⅜" miniature brick squares, four using black and five using clay paint. **Marbleize** candlestick holder using clay, med. tan, med. brown, and a few specks of black paint. Paint rims of candlestick holder using metallic gold paint.

Embellishing:

Using wood glue, glue candle cup onto candlestick holder. Glue doll pin stand onto candle cup. Glue bricks around outside edge of doll pin stand. Glue egg onto doll pin stand.

 # Dot Eggs

Pictured on page 25

Materials:

Acrylic gesso. Acrylic paint: black; dk. orange; white. Acrylic spray sealer. Eggs: wooden, 2½" (2). Paintbrushes. Sandpaper.

Painting:

Refer to General Instructions For Egg Painting on pages 7-10. Prepare eggs for painting. **Basecoat** one egg using dk. orange and one egg using black paint. **Detail** eggs referring to picture on page 25. Randomly **dot** eggs. Slightly sand each egg for worn appearance before applying spray sealer.

Plaid Egg Trio

Pictured on page 24

Materials:
Acrylic gesso. Acrylic paint: dk. blue; dk. brown; gold; dk. green; dk. red; off-white. Acrylic spray sealer. Eggs: wooden, 2½" (3). Paintbrushes. Sandpaper.

Painting:
Refer to General Instructions For Egg Painting on pages 7-10. Prepare eggs for painting. **Basecoat** one egg using dk. red, one egg using

dk. blue, and one egg using gold paint. **Detail** eggs referring to pattern. Slightly sand each egg for worn appearance before applying spray sealer.

Brick Egg

Pictured on page 24

Materials:
Acrylic gesso. Acrylic paint: gold; red. Acrylic spray sealer. Egg: wooden, 2½". Paintbrushes. Sandpaper.

Painting:
Refer to General Instructions For Egg Painting on pages 7-10. Prepare egg for painting. **Basecoat** egg using gold paint. **Detail** egg referring to picture on page 24. Slightly sand egg for worn appearance before applying spray sealer.

Sewing Egg

Pictured on page 24

Materials:
Acrylic gesso. Acrylic paint: dk. brown; dk. green; dk. red; tan. Acrylic spray sealer. Egg: wooden, 2½". Glue: craft. Needle: large-eyed. Sewing notions: buttons, variety (7); hook; miniature scissors; snap; spool, wooden 1½"-diameter; thimble. Paintbrushes. String: natural color. Thread: pearl cotton, color of choice.

Painting:
Refer to General Instructions For Egg Painting

on pages 7-10. Refer to picture on page 24. Prepare egg for painting. **Basecoat** egg using dk. green paint. **Dry-brush** egg using dk. red, then tan paint. **Wash** spool using dk. brown paint. Apply spray sealer to egg and spool.
Embellishing:
Wrap thread around spool until completely covered. Using craft glue, glue both ends of thread to spool to secure. Glue egg to top of spool. Thread natural string onto large-eyed needle. Thread buttons, snap, and hook on string randomly. Wrap and glue thread and notions around spool. Glue thimble on top of egg. Glue miniature scissors to side of thimble.

Wax Egg

Pictured on page 24

Materials:
Candle wax. Candle wick. Coffee can: clean, empty. Egg: blown. Egg holder. Leaves: ivy. Scissors. Skewer.

Embellishing:
Refer to General Instructions Preparing Real Eggs on pages 9-10. Blow out egg. Use skewer to carefully clean out egg membranes from

inside of shell. Dry egg and place in egg holder. Make hole in top of eggshell large enough to pour wax into. Melt wax in coffee can following manufacturer's instructions. Place wick in bottom hole of egg. Pour melted wax into top of eggshell. Wax will shrink as it hardens, so continue filling egg until wax no longer shrinks. When wax is completely cool, peel shell away from wax. Hold egg by wick and dip into melted wax. Place leaves onto egg randomly. Continue dipping egg into melted wax to reach desired effect.

Cock-A-Doodle Egg
Pictured on page 25

Materials:
Acrylic gesso. Acrylic paint: black; gold; lt. gold; dk. green; dk. orange; dk. red; off-white. Acrylic spray sealer. Egg: wooden, 2½". Paintbrushes.

Painting:
Refer to General Instructions For Egg Painting on pages 7-10. Prepare egg for painting. **Basecoat** egg using gold paint. **Dry-brush** heavily using off-white paint. **Detail** egg referring to pattern. **Dot** black rooster using off-white paint. Pattern repeats around egg alternating paint colors.

Melon Egg Trio
Pictured on page 25

Materials:
Acrylic gesso. Acrylic paint: black; dk. gold; dk. green; dk. red; tan; dk. tan; white. Acrylic spray sealer. Eggs: wooden, 2½" (3). Paintbrushes.

Painting:
Refer to General Instructions For Egg Painting on pages 7-10. Prepare eggs for painting. **Basecoat** one egg using dk. gold, one egg using dk. red, and one egg using tan paint. **Detail** eggs referring to pattern.

Ladybug Egg
Pictured on page 26

Materials:
Acrylic gesso. Acrylic paint: dk. blue; dk. gray; green; lt. olive green; red; off-white. Acrylic spray sealer. Egg: wooden, 2½". Paintbrushes. Pen: fine-tip permanent, black. Toothbrush.

Painting:
Refer to General Instructions For Egg Painting on pages 7-10. Prepare egg for painting. **Basecoat** egg using green paint. **Detail** egg referring to pattern. **Splatter** egg using dk. gray paint. **Outline** egg using pen.

Cow Egg

Pictured on page 25

Materials:
Acrylic gesso. Acrylic paint: gray/tan; dk. green; dk. orange; off-white; white. Acrylic spray sealer. Egg: wooden, 2½". Paintbrushes. Sponge. Toothbrush.

Painting:
Refer to General Instructions For Egg Painting on pages 7-10. Prepare egg for painting. **Sponge** egg sparingly using dk. green paint for basecoat. **Sponge** egg heavily using off-white paint. **Detail** egg referring to pattern. **Splatter** egg with gray/tan paint.

Stenciled Name Egg

Pictured on page 25

Materials:
Acrylic gesso. Acrylic paint: dull med. blue; med. tan; off-white. Acrylic spray sealer. Egg: wooden, 2½". Paintbrushes. Spray stain: walnut. Stencil: alphabet.

Painting:
Refer to General Instructions For Egg Painting on pages 7-10. Prepare egg for painting. **Basecoat** egg using med. tan paint. **Detail** egg referring to pattern. **Stencil** name of choice using off-white paint and alphabet stencil. Lightly spray egg with walnut stain.

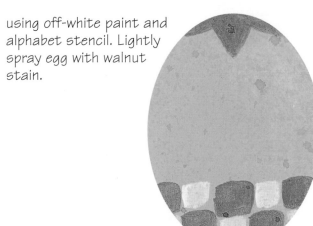

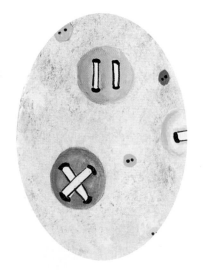

Button Egg

Pictured on page 25

Materials:
Acrylic gesso. Acrylic paint: black; dk. brown; dk. green; lt. green; dk. pink; tan; med. yellow; pale yellow; off-white. Acrylic spray sealer. Egg: wooden, 2½". Paintbrushes. Sponge.

Painting:
Refer to General Instructions For Egg Painting on pages 7-10. Prepare egg for painting. **Sponge** egg using dk. brown, tan, and off-white paint for basecoat. **Detail** egg referring to pattern. **Float** to shade large buttons using lt. green to dk. green, pale yellow to med. yellow, and dk. pink paint. **Dot** button holes using black paint.

Carrot Egg Trio

Pictured on page 26

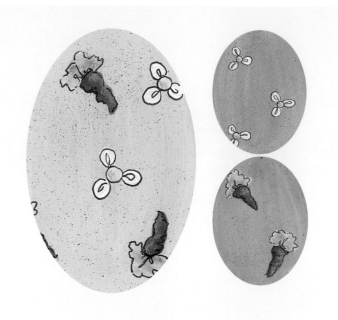

Materials:
Acrylic gesso. Acrylic paint: dk. brown; gold; dk. green; lt. green; dk. orange; lt. yellow; med. orange; tan; off-white. Acrylic spray sealer. Eggs: wooden, 2½" (3). Paintbrushes. Pen: fine-tip permanent, black.

Painting:
Refer to General Instructions For Egg Painting on pages 7-10. Prepare eggs for painting. **Basecoat** one egg using lt. green, gold, and tan; one egg using gold and tan; and one egg using tan and off-white paint. **Detail** eggs, referring to pattern. Outline egg using pen.

Crow Birdhouse Egg

Pictured on page 26

Materials:
Acrylic gesso. Acrylic paint: black; lt. blue; flesh; gold; med. green; dk. red; red/brown; med. yellow. Acrylic spray sealer. Egg: wooden, 2½". Paintbrushes. Pen: fine-tip permanent, black. Spray stain: walnut.

Painting:
Refer to General Instructions For Egg Painting on pages 7-10. Prepare egg for painting. **Basecoat** egg using gold paint. **Detail** egg, referring to pattern. Apply walnut spray stain. **Outline** egg using pen.

Stenciled Tree Egg

Pictured on page 26

Materials:
Acrylic gesso. Acrylic paint: dk. green; red; med. red/brown; med. tan; med. yellow. Acrylic spray sealer. Egg: wooden, 2½". Knife: craft. Paintbrushes. Pencil. Sponge. Spray stain: walnut. Stencil paper.

Painting:
Refer to General Instructions For Egg Painting on pages 7-10. Prepare egg for painting.

Basecoat egg using med. tan paint. Refer to Stenciled Tree Egg Patterns on page 91. Draw pattern on stencil paper and cut out with craft knife. Using sponge, **stencil** four trees, stars, trunks, and tree stands around egg. Apply walnut spray stain.

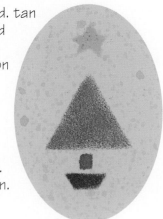

Pumpkin Sunflower Egg

Pictured on page 26

Materials

Acrylic gesso. Acrylic paint: black; dk. brown; clay; gold; med. green; very pale olive. Acrylic spray sealer. Egg: wooden, 2½". Paintbrushes. Pen: fine-tip permanent, black. Spray stain: walnut.

Painting:

Refer to General Instructions For Egg Painting

on pages 7-10. Prepare egg for painting. **Basecoat** egg using very pale olive paint. **Detail** egg referring to pattern. Apply walnut spray stain. **Outline** egg using pen.

 # Candy Hearts Egg

Pictured on page 27

Materials:

Acrylic gesso. Acrylic paint: lt. orange; pink; lt. pale pink; purple; dull rose; white. Acrylic spray sealer. Egg: wooden, 2½". Sponge. Paintbrushes. Pen: fine-tip permanent, black.

Painting:

Refer to General Instructions For Egg Painting

on pages 7-10. Prepare egg for painting. **Basecoat** egg using lt. pale pink paint. **Sponge** egg using white, then dull rose paint. **Detail** egg referring to pattern. **Outline** hearts using pen.

Rosebuds Egg

Pictured on page 27

Materials:

Acrylic gesso. Acrylic paint: lt. brown; lt. green; med. green; med. pink; lt. pink; med. purple; lt. tan. Acrylic spray sealer. Egg: wooden, 2½". Paintbrushes. Pen: fine-tip permanent, black. Spray stain: walnut.

Painting:

Refer to General Instructions For Egg Painting on pages 7-10. Prepare egg for painting. **Basecoat** egg using lt. tan paint. Apply spray stain. **Detail** egg referring to pattern. **Outline** egg using pen.

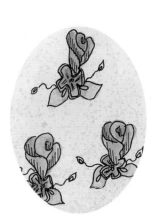

Birthday Present Egg

Pictured on page 27

Materials:

Acrylic gesso. Acrylic paint: lt. blue; pale blue; pale flesh; green; lt. green; dull mauve; purple; rose; violet; lt. dull yellow; dk. yellow. Acrylic spray sealer. Egg: wooden, 2½". Paintbrushes. Pen: fine-tip permanent, black.

Painting:

Refer to General Instructions For Egg Painting

on pages 7-10. Prepare egg for painting. **Basecoat** egg using pale flesh paint. **Watercolor** egg referring to pattern. Flower pattern is repeated around each side of present. **Outline** egg using pen.

Cupcake Egg

Pictured on page 27

Materials:

Acrylic gesso. Acrylic paint: lt. blue; pale blue; lt. brown; green; lt. olive green; dull mauve, pale pink; rose; tan; white; yellow; mustard yellow. Acrylic spray sealer. Egg: wooden, 2½". Paintbrushes. Pen: fine-tip permanent, black.

Painting:

Refer to General Instructions For Egg Painting on pages 7-10. Prepare egg for painting. **Basecoat** egg using mustard yellow paint. **Watercolor** egg referring to pattern. **Outline** egg using pen.

Painted Flowers Egg

Pictured on page 27

Materials:

Acrylic gesso. Acrylic paint: dk. blue; dk. green; lt. green; pale pink; dk. red; off-white. Acrylic spray sealer. Egg: wooden, 2½". Paintbrushes. Pen: fine-tip permanent, black.

Painting:

Refer to General Instructions For Egg Painting on pages 7-10. Prepare egg for painting. **Basecoat** egg using pale pink paint. **Detail** egg referring to pattern. **Outline** egg using pen.

Stamped Eggs

Pictured on page 27

Materials:

Acrylic gesso. Acrylic paint: lt. gold; green; very pale yellow. Acrylic spray sealer. Eggs: wooden, 2½" (2). Embossing ink. Embossing powder: green. Paintbrushes. Rubber stamps: leaf; basket weave, ½". Sponge.

Painting:

Refer to General Instructions For Egg Painting on pages 7-10. Prepare eggs for painting. **Sponge** eggs using lt. gold paint for basecoat. **Sponge** eggs using very pale yellow paint. **Stamp** eggs referring to picture on page 28. Apply embossing powder. **Detail** vines using green paint.

Bird & Heart Egg

Pictured on page 27

Materials:

Acrylic gesso. Acrylic paint: black; dk. blue; lt. blue; gold; dk. pink; pale yellow; very pale yellow. Acrylic spray sealer. Egg: wooden, 2½". Sponge.

Painting:

Refer to General Instructions For Egg Painting on pages 7-10. Prepare egg for painting. **Sponge** egg using very pale yellow paint for basecoat. **Basecoat** bird using lt. blue paint referring to pattern. **Float** bird using dk. blue paint. **Float** hearts using dk. pink paint. **Outline** bird and hearts using black paint.

Dove Egg

Pictured on page 27

Materials:
Acrylic gesso. Acrylic paint: pale pink; dk. rose; dk. tan; off-white; white. Acrylic spray sealer. Egg: wooden, 2½". Paintbrushes. Pen: fine-tip permanent, black. Sponge.

Painting:
Refer to General Instructions For Egg Painting

on pages 7-10. Prepare egg for painting. **Basecoat** egg using pale pink paint. **Sponge** egg using white paint. **Detail** egg referring to pattern. Heart pattern is repeated around egg. **Outline** egg using pen.

Noah's Ark Egg

Pictured on page 27

Materials:
Egg: hard-boiled. Food coloring: blue; green; red; yellow. Icing gel/concentrated paste: black. Paintbrushes. Water.

Painting:
Refer to General Instructions for Preparing Real Eggs and Painting Techniques on pages 9-10.

Colors can be modified by diluting with water or adding additional color. Use non-diluted color for shading. **Basecoat** egg using diluted blue food coloring for sky and sea. **Detail** egg referring to pattern using diluted food coloring. **Outline** egg using black icing gel/concentrated paste.

Log Cabin Egg

Pictured on page 28

Materials:
Acrylic gesso. Acrylic paint: dk. brown; cream; gray/green; green; dk. green; orange; tan; yellow. Acrylic spray sealer. Egg: wooden, 2½". Paintbrushes.

Painting:
Refer to General Instructions For Egg Painting

on pages 7-10. Prepare egg for painting. **Basecoat** egg using tan paint. **Basecoat** grass using green paint. **Detail** egg referring to pattern. **Float** tiles on roof using dk. green paint.

Country Home Egg

Pictured on page 28

Materials:
Acrylic gesso. Acrylic paint: lt. blue; cream; green; red; slate. Acrylic spray sealer. Bird: wooden, 1". Dowel: wooden ³⁄₁₆" x 3¼". Drill with ³⁄₁₆" bit. Egg: wooden, 2½". Glue: craft. Paintbrushes. Knife: craft. Wood: ¼" thick, 1½" square.

Painting:
Refer to General Instructions For Egg Painting on pages 7-10. Prepare egg for painting.

Basecoat egg using cream paint. **Detail** egg and bird referring to pattern.
Embellishing:
Drill ³⁄₁₆" hole in center of egg for perch; wide end of egg and center of wood square for stand. Cut dowel ¾" long for perch and 2½" long for stand. Using craft glue, secure perch and stand into place. Glue bird onto perch.

Igloo Egg

Pictured on page 28

Materials:
Acrylic gesso. Acrylic paint: black; blue/green; med. blue; gray/blue; orange; white; yellow. Acrylic spray sealer. Egg: wooden, 2½". Paintbrushes.

Painting:
Refer to General Instructions For Egg Painting on pages 7-10. Prepare egg for painting. **Basecoat** egg using white paint. **Detail** egg referring to pattern.

Thatch Cottage Egg

Pictured on page 28

Materials:
Acrylic gesso. Acrylic paint: pale blue; gray; green; pink; red; tan; white; yellow. Acrylic spray sealer. Egg: wooden, 2½". Paintbrushes. Sponge.

Painting:
Refer to General Instructions For Egg Painting on pages 7-10. Prepare egg for painting. **Basecoat** egg using white paint. **Detail** egg referring to pattern. **Float** under roof, windows, and sides of house using gray paint. **Sponge** flowers using pink, pale blue, yellow, and red paint.

 # Flowerpot Eggs

Pictured on page 28

Materials:
Acrylic gesso. Acrylic paint: clay; flesh; gold; dk. green; med. green; lt. ivory; purple; dull purple; dk. red; tan; dk. tan; lt. tan; off-white. Acrylic spray sealer. Eggs: wooden, 2½"; 1½". Flowerpots: wooden, 2½"; 1½". Sponge. Spray stain: walnut. Paintbrushes. Pen: fine-tip, permanent, black.

Painting:
Refer to General Instructions For Egg Painting on pages 7-10. Prepare eggs and flowerpots for painting. **Basecoat** eggs using lt. ivory paint. **Sponge** eggs using flesh paint. **Watercolor** eggs referring to pattern. Apply walnut spray stain. **Outline** eggs using pen. **Basecoat** flowerpots using dk. tan paint. **Stipple** flowerpots using clay then gold paint. **Outline** flowerpots using pen.

Birdhouse Egg

Pictured on page 28

Materials:
Acrylic gesso. Acrylic paint: clay; dk. blue; gold; green; dk. green; med. purple; red; very pale yellow. Acrylic spray sealer. Egg: wooden, 2½". Paintbrushes. Stamp: small check.

Painting:
Refer to General Instructions For Egg Painting on pages 7-10. Prepare egg for painting. **Basecoat** top three-fourths of egg using very pale yellow and bottom one-fourth of egg using green diluted paint. **Stamp** checks on egg using diluted clay paint. **Basecoat** roof, house, flowers, and leaves using diluted paint, referring to pattern. **Detail** egg referring to pattern. **Float** to shade roof, house, flowers, and leaves using non-diluted colors.

Piece of Cake Egg

Pictured on page 29

Materials:
Acrylic gesso. Acrylic paint: blue; lt. blue; pale blue; lt. brown; green; lt. moss green, dull mauve; pale pink; purple; rose; tan; violet; mustard yellow. Acrylic spray sealer. Egg: wooden, 4½". Paintbrushes. Pen: fine-tip permanent, black. Toothbrush.

Painting:
Refer to General Instructions For Egg Painting on pages 7-10. Prepare egg for painting. **Basecoat** egg using lt. moss green paint. **Splatter** egg using green paint. **Watercolor** egg referring to pattern. **Outline** egg using pen.

Rose Birdhouse Egg

Pictured on page 29

Materials:
Acrylic gesso. Acrylic paint: lt. brown; dk. green; lt. green; dull mauve; very pale mauve; purple; dull purple; lt. rose; dk. tan; lt. tan; very pale off-white. Acrylic spray sealer. Egg: wooden, 4½". Paintbrushes. Pen: fine-tip permanent, black. Sponge. Spray stain: walnut.

Painting:
Refer to General Instructions For Egg Painting on pages 7-10. Prepare egg for painting. **Basecoat** egg using lt. tan paint. **Sponge** egg using lt. brown paint. **Watercolor** egg referring to pattern. Apply walnut spray stain. **Outline** egg using pen.

Watering Can Egg

Pictured on page 29

Materials:
Acrylic gesso. Acrylic paint: gold; gray; green; red; dk. tan; dk. yellow; off-white; white. Acrylic spray sealer. Egg: wooden, 4½". Paintbrushes. Pen: fine-tip permanent, black. Spray stain: walnut. Toothbrush.

Painting:
Refer to General Instructions For Egg Painting on pages 7-10. Prepare egg for painting. **Basecoat** egg using dk. yellow paint. **Splatter**

egg using off-white paint. Lightly apply walnut spray stain. **Detail** egg referring to pattern. **Outline** egg using pen.

Flower Button Egg

Pictured on page 29

Materials:
Acrylic gesso. Acrylic paint: black; dk. blue; med. brown; clay; med. gold; dk. green; red; off-white; very pale yellow. Acrylic spray sealer. Antique medium. Egg: wooden, 2½". Paintbrushes.

Painting:
Refer to General Instructions For Egg Painting on pages 7-10. Prepare egg for painting. **Basecoat** egg using off-white paint. Apply **antique** medium. **Watercolor** egg referring to

pattern. **Detail** egg referring to pattern. **Float** to shade egg with non-diluted paint. **Outline** egg using black paint.

Star & Fish Egg

Pictured on page 29

Materials:
Acrylic gesso. Acrylic paint: med. blue; med. blue/green; lt. gold; dk. red; off-white; med. yellow/green. Acrylic spray sealer. Egg: wooden, 2½". Paintbrushes. Pen: fine-tip permanent, black.

Painting:
Refer to General Instructions For Egg Painting on pages 7-10. Prepare egg for painting. **Sponge** egg using med. blue paint for basecoat. **Sponge** egg very sparingly using med. blue/green paint. **Detail** egg referring to pattern. **Outline** egg using pen.

I Love You Egg

Pictured on page 29

Materials:
Acrylic gesso. Acrylic paint: pale blue; flesh; green; lt. pink; dk. red; tan; off-white. Acrylic spray sealer. Egg: wooden, 1½". Paintbrushes. Pen: fine-tip permanent, black.

Painting:
Refer to General Instructions For Egg Painting on pages 7-10. Prepare egg for painting. **Basecoat** egg using pale blue paint. **Watercolor** egg referring to pattern. **Outline** egg using pen.

Cat & Moon Egg

Pictured on page 29

Materials:
Acrylic gesso. Acrylic paint: black; med. blue; clay; gold; very pale yellow. Acrylic spray sealer. Egg: wooden, 2½". Paintbrushes. Sponge.

Painting:
Refer to General Instructions For Egg Painting on pages 7-10. Prepare egg for painting. **Sponge** egg lightly using med. blue paint for basecoat. **Sponge** egg using very pale yellow paint. **Detail** egg referring to pattern. **Float** to highlight stars using very pale yellow paint. **Float** to shade cat using gold paint.

Watermelon Egg

Pictured on page 29

Materials:
Acrylic gesso. Acrylic paint: black; gold; dk. green; lt. green; red; very pale yellow; yellow/green. Acrylic spray sealer. Egg: wooden, 2½". Paintbrushes. Sandpaper. Sponge. Water.

Painting:
Refer to General Instructions For Egg Painting on pages 7-10. Prepare egg for painting. **Sponge** egg lightly using red paint. **Sponge** egg heavily using very pale yellow paint. **Detail** checks around top and bottom of egg using diluted gold paint. Slightly sand egg for worn appearance. **Watercolor** egg referring to pattern. Using non-diluted paint, **float** to shade egg using red on red and dk. green on lt. green paint. **Outline** egg using black paint.

Eggciting For Christmas

Candy Cane Egg

Pictured on page 30

Materials:
Acrylic gesso. Acrylic paint gold; dk. green; med. green; red; tan; dk. tan; off-white. Acrylic spray sealer. Egg: wooden, 2½". Paintbrushes. Pen: fine-tip permanent, black. Sponge.

Painting:
Refer to General Instructions For Egg Painting on pages 7-10. Prepare egg for painting. **Basecoat** egg using tan paint. **Sponge** egg lightly using dk. tan paint. **Watercolor** egg referring to pattern. **Outline** egg using pen.

Stocking Egg

Pictured on page 30

Materials:
Acrylic gesso. Acrylic paint: dk. blue; lt. blue; lt. brown; med. brown; dk. gray; green; dk. tan; lt. tan; red; med. red/brown; very dk. red; off-white; very pale off-white. Acrylic spray sealer. Egg: wooden, 2½". Paintbrushes. Pen: fine-tip permanent, black. Sponge.

Painting:
Refer to General Instructions For Egg Painting on pages 7-10. Prepare egg for painting. **Basecoat** egg using dk. tan paint. **Sponge** egg using lt. tan paint. **Detail** egg referring to pattern. **Outline** egg using pen.

Patches Egg

Pictured on page 30

Materials:
Acrylic gesso. Acrylic paint: black; dk. brown; lt. gold; green; dk. green; red; off-white; pale yellow. Acrylic spray sealer. Egg: wooden, 2½". Paintbrushes.

Painting:
Refer to General Instructions For Egg Painting on pages 7-10. Prepare egg for painting. **Basecoat** egg using pale yellow and lt. gold paint. **Detail** egg referring to pattern. **Outline** egg using black paint.

Stars Egg

Pictured on page 30

Materials:
Acrylic gesso. Acrylic paint: black; lt. brown; med. brown; tan; very pale yellow. Acrylic spray sealer. Paintbrushes. Egg: wooden, 2½". Sponge. Toothbrush.

Painting:
Refer to General Instructions For Egg Painting on pages 7-10. Prepare egg for painting. **Basecoat** egg using very pale yellow paint. **Sponge** around outside, top, and bottom of egg

using lt. brown paint, leaving center on front and back yellow. **Detail** egg referring to pattern. **Outline** stars using black paint. **Splatter** egg using med. brown paint.

Bunny in a Pocket Egg

Pictured on page 30

Materials:
Acrylic gesso. Acrylic paint: dk. blue; brown; lt. brown; pale flesh; gold; dk. gray; green; dk. green; lt. green; pale mauve; purple; red; dk. red; rose; dk. tan; lt. tan; pale off-white; lt. yellow. Acrylic spray sealer. Egg: wooden, 4½". Paintbrushes. Pen: fine-tip permanent, black. Sponge. Spray stain: walnut. Water.

Painting:
Refer to General Instructions For Egg Painting on pages 7-10. Prepare egg for painting. **Basecoat** egg using dk. green paint. **Sponge** egg

using lt. tan paint. **Detail** egg referring to pattern. Cheeks and inside ears are painted with diluted rose paint. Plaid patch is painted with diluted pale mauve paint. Apply walnut spray stain. **Outline** egg using pen.

Frosty the Snowman Egg

Pictured on page 30

Materials:
Acrylic gesso. Acrylic paint: black; blue; dk. green; lt. green; gray; orange; red; white; lt. yellow; med. yellow. Acrylic spray sealer. Egg: wooden, 4½". Paintbrushes. Sponge. Water.

Painting:
Refer to General Instructions For Egg Painting on pages 7-10. Prepare egg for painting. **Sponge** egg using blue paint. **Detail** egg referring to pattern. Use slightly diluted paint on snowman and heart. Use non-diluted paint for plaid inside heart. **Stipple** cheeks using red paint.

Snowflake Snowman Egg

Pictured on page 30

Materials:
Acrylic gesso. Acrylic paint: dk. blue; dk. gray; dk. green; red; white. Acrylic spray sealer. Egg: wooden, 4½". Paintbrushes. Pen: fine-tip permanent, black. Toothbrush. Water.

Painting:
Refer to General Instructions For Egg Painting on pages 7-10. Prepare egg for painting. **Basecoat** egg using dk. blue paint. **Splatter** egg using white paint. **Detail** egg referring to pattern. **Float** around edge of snowman using diluted dk. blue paint. **Float** under snowman for snow using white paint. **Outline** egg using pen.

Christmas Tree Egg

Pictured on page 30

Materials:
Acrylic gesso. Acrylic paint: black; brown; dk. green; lt. green; red; med. yellow; very pale yellow. Acrylic spray sealer. Egg: wooden, 4½". Paintbrushes. Sponge. Water.

Painting:
Refer to General Instructions For Egg Painting on pages 7-10. Prepare egg for painting. **Sponge** egg using med. yellow paint for basecoat. **Sponge** egg using very pale yellow paint to soften. **Detail** egg referring to pattern. Using slightly diluted paint, **float** tree using dk. green, heart using red, trunk using brown, and button using very pale yellow paint. **Outline** egg using black paint.

Heart & Star Egg

Pictured on page 30

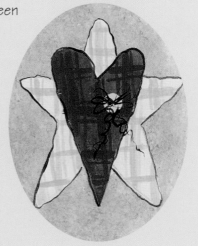

Materials:
Acrylic gesso. Acrylic paint: black; dk. green; lt. green; red; med. yellow; pale yellow. Acrylic spray sealer. Egg: wooden, 4½". Sponge.

Painting:
Refer to General Instructions For Egg Painting on pages 7-10. Prepare egg for painting. **Sponge** egg using dk. green paint for basecoat. **Sponge** egg using lt. green then pale yellow paint to soften. **Detail** egg referring to pattern. **Stipple** button using dk. green paint. **Dot** button holes on button using black paint. **Outline** egg using black paint.

Father Christmas Egg

Pictured on page 31

Materials:
Acrylic gesso. Acrylic paint: black; dk. blue; lt. blue; dk. brown; flesh; gray; orange; red; tan; yellow; white. Acrylic spray sealer. Egg: wooden, 4½". Paintbrushes.

Painting:
Refer to General Instructions For Egg Painting on pages 7-10. Prepare egg for painting. **Detail** egg referring to pattern. **Float** under hood, sleeves, sack, and down front of jacket using dk. brown paint. **Float** under teddy's face, arms, and eye area using tan paint. **Float** under gloves using black paint. **Float** eyebrows using white paint. **Dot** eyes using black then white paint.

Teddy Bear Egg

Pictured on page 31

Materials:
Acrylic gesso. Acrylic paint: black; dk. red; med. reddish brown; med. tan; white. Acrylic spray sealer. Egg: wooden, 4½". Felt: dk. brown; lt. brown; green; red. Glue: hot glue gun and glue sticks. Paintbrushes. Scissors. Sock: red.

Painting:
Refer to General Instructions For Egg Painting on pages 7-10. Prepare egg for painting. **Detail** egg referring to pattern. **Stipple** cheeks using dk. red paint.

Embellishing:
Refer to picture on page 31. Cut red sock off at ankle. Fold one end up ¼", fold again about 1". Pull a thread out of sock and use it to tie top of stocking hat closed. Using hot glue gun and glue stick, hot-glue hat onto top of egg. Refer to Teddy Bear Egg Patterns on page 92. Cut out two large ears from dk. brown felt for outer ear. Cut out two small ears from lt. brown felt for inner ear. Cut out two holly leaves from green felt and three berries from red felt. Hot-glue small ears to large ears. Hot-glue ears to hat. Hot-glue holly leaves and berries to hat. **Comma stroke** berries using white paint.

Tissue Paper Tree Egg

Pictured on page 31

Materials
Acrylic gesso. Acrylic paint: white. Egg: papier mâché, 6". Glue: découpage. Hole punch. Paintbrush. Tissue paper: gold; green; lilac; red; teal.

Painting:
Refer to General Instructions For Egg Painting on pages 7-10. Prepare egg for painting. **Basecoat** egg using white paint.

Embellishing:
Refer to Tissue Paper Tree Egg Patterns on page 92. Fan fold green tissue paper twelve times using a ¾" length fold 3" high. Trace tree pattern on the fold and hand-tear six tree patterns. Fan fold red tissue paper six times. Trace pot pattern on the fold and hand-tear six pot patterns. Fan fold five pieces of teal tissue paper and one piece of gold tissue paper together. Trace star pattern on the fold and hand-tear six star patterns. Using hole punch, punch out round ornaments from red and lilac tissue papers. Refer to picture on page 31. Coat egg with layer of découpage glue. Glue tissue paper trees, pots, stars, and round ornaments onto egg.

Stacked Tree Eggs

Pictured on page 31

Materials:
Acrylic gesso. Acrylic paint: dk. green; dk. red; yellow. Acrylic spray sealer. Dowels: wooden, ⅛" x 6"; ³⁄₁₆" x 3". Drill with ⅛" and ³⁄₁₆" bits. Eggs: wooden, 2½"; 1½"; ⅞". Flowerpot: wooden, 1½" tall. Garland: miniature beaded. Glue of choice. Knife: craft. Paintbrushes. Ribbon: ⅜"-wide plaid, 14". Plaster: quick drying. Spanish moss. Star: wooden, 1".

Painting:
Refer to General Instructions For Egg Painting on pages 7-10. Drill ⅛" hole through small and middle sized eggs. Drill ⅛" hole into top of large egg. Drill ³⁄₁₆" hole in bottom of large egg. Push ⅛" dowel into top of large egg. Thread middle egg followed by small egg onto ⅛" dowel. Using craft knife, trim top of ⅛" dowel to ¼". Prepare eggs, dowels, star, and flowerpot for painting. **Basecoat** eggs and dowels using dk. green paint. **Basecoat** flowerpot using dk. red paint. **Basecoat** star using yellow paint. Leave bottom ³⁄₁₆" dowel unpainted.

Embellishing:
Refer to picture on page 31. Using glue of choice, push and glue ³⁄₁₆" dowel into bottom of large egg. Trim ³⁄₁₆" dowel to 2½". Mix plaster, following manufacturer's instructions. Fill flowerpot with plaster. Place ³⁄₁₆" dowel, with tree upright, into plaster and allow to dry. Glue star on top of ⅛" dowel. Wrap and glue tree with beaded garland. Glue moss in flowerpot to cover plaster. Wrap ribbon around flowerpot and tie into small bow.

Paper Reindeer Egg

Pictured on page 31

Materials:
Acrylic gesso. Acrylic paint: white. Egg: papier mâché, 6". Eye screw: small. Glue: craft. Hole punch. Paintbrush. Paper: gift wrap, metallic red; handmade, brown. Pencil. Tape: masking. Ribbon: ½"-wide plaid, 54". Scissors: fabric.

Painting:
Refer to General Instructions For Egg Painting on pages 7-10. Prepare egg for painting. **Basecoat** egg using white paint.

Embellishing:
Refer to Paper Reindeer Egg Patterns on page 92. Fold 5" square piece of brown paper in half. Trace reindeer head pattern on the fold of brown paper and hand-tear three reindeer head patterns. Using hole punch, punch out holes for eyes. Refer to picture on page 31. Place reindeer heads on egg with masking tape for spacing. Using craft glue, secure reindeer heads onto egg. Trace and hand-tear three nose patterns from metallic red paper. Glue noses onto reindeer heads. Cut three 12" lengths of ribbon. Make three bows. Glue under reindeer heads. Attach eye screw into top of egg. For hanging, tie remaining ribbon to eye screw, winding through eye screw twice to hide screw.

 # Santa & Holly Egg

Pictured on page 33

Materials:
Acrylic gesso. Acrylic paint: med. flesh; very pale flesh; dk. green; pink; red; dk. red; dk. reddish brown; dk. tan; off-white; very pale off-white. Acrylic spray sealer. Egg: wooden, 4½". Paintbrushes. Pen: fine-tip permanent, black. Spray stain: walnut.

Painting:
Refer to General Instructions For Egg Painting on pages 7-10. Prepare egg for painting. **Basecoat** egg using very pale flesh paint. **Watercolor** egg referring to pattern. Apply walnut spray stain. **Outline** egg using pen.

Ornament Egg Trio

Pictured on page 32

Materials:
Acrylic gesso. Acrylic paint: black; green; red; metallic silver; white; yellow. Acrylic spray sealer. Baking clay: white. Eggs: wooden, 2½" (3). Glitter spray: silver. Glue of choice. Knife: craft. Needlenose pliers. Paintbrushes. Toothpicks. Water. Wire: ⅙"-gauge, black, 3". Wire cutters.

Painting:
Refer to General Instructions For Egg Painting and Sculpting Baking Clay on pages 7-10. Prepare eggs for painting. **Basecoat** one egg using green, one egg using red, and one egg using yellow paint. Dilute white paint with water. **Detail** white over green, red and yellow eggs for highlight referring to pattern. Apply glitter spray to each egg.

Embellishing:
Sculpt clay into three ornament holders. Using dull side of craft knife, make indentations on each holder. Using toothpick, place two holes in each holder ¼" apart for wire placement. Bake clay, following manufacturer's instructions. **Basecoat** clay pieces using metallic silver paint. **Wash** clay pieces using black paint. Cut wire into three 1" lengths. Using needlenose pliers, bend and glue wire into holes in each holder. Using glue of choice, secure each holder to wide end of each egg.

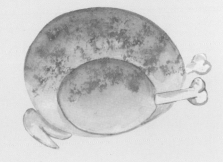

Acorn Egg

Pictured on page 32

Materials:
Acrylic gesso. Acrylic paint: lt. brown; med. brown; dk. green. Acrylic spray sealer. Antique medium. Baking clay: white, 4-oz. pkg. Egg: wooden, 2½". Glue of choice. Knife: craft. Paintbrushes. Rag: soft. Toothpick.

Painting:
Refer to General Instructions For Egg Painting and Sculpting Baking Clay on pages 7-10. Sculpt clay into acorn cap, leaf, and stem, referring to picture on page 32. Using craft knife, score acorn cap into four equal sections. Using paintbrush end, make rows of indentations. Using toothpick, make veins in leaf. Bake clay pieces, following manufacturer's instructions. Prepare egg and clay pieces for painting. **Basecoat** egg using lt. brown, acorn cap using med. brown, and leaf using dk. green paint. Using soft rag, apply **antique** medium to all pieces.

Embellishing:
Using glue of choice, secure acorn cap, leaf, and stem on top of egg.

Turkey Egg

Pictured on page 32

Materials:
Acrylic gesso. Acrylic paint: cream; flesh; reddish brown. Acrylic spray sealer. Baking clay: flesh colored. Dowel: wooden, ³⁄₁₆" x 3". Egg: wooden, 2½". Glue: craft. Knife: craft. Paintbrushes.

Painting:
Refer to General Instructions For Egg Painting and Sculpting Baking Clay on pages 7-10. Cut dowel into two 1½" lengths. Sculpt clay for two leg bone ends, two drumsticks, and two wings. Bake clay, following manufacturer's instructions. Using craft glue, glue dowels into drumstick to form legs. Glue leg bone ends onto dowels. Glue wings and drumsticks onto egg. Prepare egg and clay pieces for painting. **Basecoat** egg and clay pieces using flesh and dowels using cream paint. **Stipple** reddish brown paint over egg, leg bones, drumsticks, and wings, referring to pattern.

Cheese Eggs

Pictured on page 32

Materials:
Acrylic gesso. Acrylic paint: med. gold; pale gold; very pale gold. Acrylic spray sealer. Eggs: wooden, 2½"; 2". Glue: craft. Mice: miniature (5). Paintbrush.

Painting:
Refer to General Instructions For Egg Painting on pages 7-10. Prepare eggs for painting. **Basecoat** eggs using very pale gold paint. **Detail** eggs using pale gold paint to make circles referring to pattern. Make "C" shape on circles using med. gold paint.

Embellishing:
Glue miniature mice on eggs as desired.

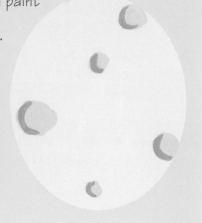

Plum Pudding Egg

Pictured on page 32

Materials:
Acrylic gesso. Acrylic paint: dk. brown; lt. brown; med. brown; cream; white. Acrylic spray sealer. Egg: wooden, 2½". Glue: craft. Holly: sprig with berries. Paintbrushes.

Painting:
Refer to General Instructions For Egg Painting on pages 7-10. Prepare egg for painting. **Basecoat** top of egg using white and bottom of egg using dk. brown paint. **Detail** egg referring to pattern. **Float** bottom of white area using cream paint.

Embellishing:
Glue holly sprig onto top of egg.

Rudolph Egg

Pictured on page 32

Materials:
Acrylic gesso. Acrylic paint: black; brown; lt. brown; metallic gold; red; white. Acrylic spray sealer. Ball: wooden, ½". Doll hair: curly, brown, 6". Egg: wooden, 3½". Felt: med brown; lt. brown; green. Garland: miniature Christmas lights, 24". Glitter spray: silver. Glue: hot glue gun and glue sticks. Paintbrushes. Scissors. Wreath: artificial, green, 2".

Painting:
Refer to General Instructions For Egg Painting on pages 7-10. Prepare egg and wooden ball for painting. **Basecoat** egg using lt. brown paint. **Detail** egg referring to pattern, with wide end as top of egg. **Dry-brush** egg using brown paint. **Wash** cheeks using red paint. **Dot** eyes using black, then white paint. Using hot glue gun and glue stick, hot-glue green felt centered over cheeks for harness. **Dot** onto green harness using metallic gold paint. **Basecoat** wooden ball, for nose, using red paint. **Comma stroke** nose using white paint.

Embellishing:
Hot-glue nose onto green harness. Refer to Rudolph Egg Patterns on page 91. Cut out two ears from lt. brown felt. Cut out two antlers from med. brown felt. Hot-glue ears, antlers, and doll hair to egg. Hot-glue egg onto wreath. Hot-glue garland randomly around egg and wreath. Lightly apply silver glitter spray.

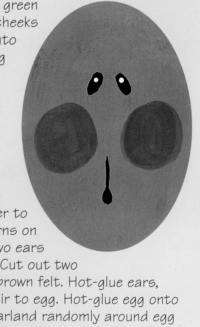

Sponged Tree Eggs

Pictured on page 33

Materials:
Acrylic gesso. Acrylic paint: dk. green; lt. green; ivory. Acrylic spray sealer. Drill with ³⁄₁₆" bit. Eggs: wooden, 2½"; 1½"; ⅞". Fiber mâché: variegated gold (1 pkg). Flowerpot: wooden, 1½". Garland: gold beaded with star. Glue of choice. Paintbrushes. Sponge. Star: wooden, 2½"-3" for base of tree. Wire: 18-gauge, floral. Wire cutters.

Painting:
Refer to General Instructions For Egg Painting on pages 7-10. Drill ³⁄₁₆" hole in base of each egg and slightly off-center in top of 2½" and 1½" eggs. Drill hole in center of star base. Prepare eggs for painting. **Sponge** eggs using dk. green paint for basecoat. **Sponge** eggs using lt. green then ivory paint.

Embellishing:
Refer to picture on page 33. Using wire cutters, cut one 1¾" length, one 1" length, and one ½" length of wire. Using glue of choice, secure 1¾" length of wire into drilled hole in center of star base. Mix fiber mâché, following manufacturer's instructions. Cover base of star using fiber mâché. Let fiber mâché dry thoroughly. Glue one end of 1" length of wire into drilled hole in top of 2½" egg and other end of wire in base of 1½" egg. Glue one end of ½" length of wire into top of 1½" egg and other end of wire in base of ⅞" egg. Apply spray sealer to eggs. Glue assembled tree onto wire on base of 3" star. Wrap garland around tree with star on top.

Scarf Snowman Egg

Pictured on page 33

Materials:
Acrylic gesso. Acrylic paint: lt. brown; dk. gray; red/brown; off-white. Acrylic spray sealer. Baking clay: white, 3 pkgs. Buttons: wooden, ¾"-wide (2). Drill with bit diameter of twigs. Egg: wooden, 4½". Glue: craft. Knife: craft. Paintbrushes. Rag. Stain: fruitwood, water-based. Twigs (2).

Painting:
Refer to General Instructions For Egg Painting and Sculpting Baking Clay on pages 7-10. Refer to picture on page 33. Sculpt clay into snowman's head, scarf, hat, hat brim, nose, and two eyes. Make impressions in clay on scarf, hat brim, and nose using dull side of craft knife. Bake clay pieces, following manufacturer's instructions. Drill holes in side of egg for twig arms. Prepare egg and clay pieces for painting. **Basecoat** egg and head using off-white paint. **Detail** egg and clay pieces referring to picture on page 33.

Embellishing:
Using craft glue, glue clay pieces and buttons to egg. Apply fruitwood stain to snowman. Wipe off excess stain. Using craft glue, insert and secure twigs for arms.

Christmas Scene Egg

Pictured on page 33

Materials:
Acrylic paint: black; metallic lt. blue; dk. green; orange; white. Beads: seed, red (33). Buttons: ceramic house, 1" (2). Egg: plastic with front opening, 4". Glue: hot glue gun and glue sticks. Garland: miniature, green, 32". Knife: pallet. Napkin ring: wooden, 1⅝" for holder. Paintbrushes. Scissors. Snowman: wooden, with hat, ¾". Sponge: small, soft. Texture medium: snow; smooth. Trees: pine with snow, 1"; 1½"; 2".

Painting:
Paint inside of egg using metallic lt. blue paint. Dampen sponge and cover outside of egg using snow texture, following manufacturer's instructions. Let snow texture dry thoroughly. **Detail** snowman referring to picture on page 33. **Basecoat** napkin ring holder using dk. green paint.

Embellishing:
Using pallet knife, apply smooth texture medium, following manufacturer's instructions, inside bottom of egg, filling to opening of egg. Place pine trees, ceramic houses, and snowman in smooth texture while still wet. Allow to dry overnight. Using hot glue gun and glue stick, hot-glue 10" of garland around edge of egg opening. Hot-glue beads in groups of three onto garland. Wrap and hot-glue garland around napkin ring for holder. Cut off excess garland.

75

Wire Angel Egg

Pictured on page 33

Materials:
Acrylic gesso. Acrylic paint: black; dk. brown; flesh; med. gold; dk. green; dk. red; white. Acrylic spray sealer. Drill with ³⁄₁₆" bit. Egg: wooden, 2½". Glue: craft; wood. Hearts: wooden, 3" (2). Paintbrushes. Pliers. Screws: small (2). Screwdriver. Stars: wooden, ¾" (5); 1⅛" (2). Wire: 18-gauge, bailing, 2 yds. Wire cutters.

Painting:
Refer to General Instructions For Egg Painting on pages 7-10. Prepare egg, stars, and hearts for painting. **Basecoat** egg using flesh, stars using med. gold, and hearts using dk. red paint. **Detail** egg and two ¾" stars, referring to picture on page 33. **Dot** eyes using black paint. **Stipple** cheeks using dk. red paint. **Wash** stars using dk. brown paint.

Embellishing:
Randomly drill 23 holes in top half of egg for wire hair and two holes in back of egg to attach wooden hearts for wings. Drill hole in each upper side of wooden hearts. Drill hole through center of one large star and three small stars. Cut twenty-three 3" lengths of wire. Bend wire into curls, leaving ³⁄₈"-½" tail. Using craft glue, secure wire into drilled holes on top of egg for hair. Using wood glue, glue large star on one heart and two ¾" detailed stars on other heart. Screw points of each heart into back of egg. Cut one 12" length of wire. Thread wire through one drilled hole in upper side of heart. Twist end of wire to secure. Twist wire, adding remaining stars onto wire. Thread wire through drilled hole in other heart. Twist end of wire to secure.

Snow Angel Egg

Pictured on page 33

Materials:
Acrylic gesso. Acrylic paint: black; flesh. Acrylic spray sealer. Awl. Ball: wooden, flat bottom, 1¼". Egg: wooden, 2½". Eye screw: ¹⁵⁄₃₂". Flowers and greenery: dried assortment. Glue: hot glue gun and glue sticks. Paintbrushes. Ribbons: 2"-wide gold elan, 11"; ¾"-wide gold metallic wire-edged, 24". Texture medium: snow. Trim: gold metallic estaz, 10", for hanger. Wire: 26-gauge. Wire cutters.

Painting:
Cover egg using snow texture, following manufacturer's instructions. Refer to picture on page 33. Form grooves on egg using end of paintbrush. Let snow texture dry thoroughly. Refer to General Instructions For Egg Painting on pages 7-10. Prepare wooden ball for painting. **Basecoat** wooden ball using flesh paint. **Detail** face on wooden ball using black paint.

Embellishing:
Using awl, pierce hole in top of wooden ball and attach eye screw. Using hot glue gun and glue stick, hot-glue flat part of wooden ball to large end of egg. Cut 2"-wide elan into two 5½" lengths for wings. Fold each 5½" length in half. Wrap end of elan with small piece of wire. Repeat with other length of elan. Cut 12" piece of wire. Starting in center, wrap wire around end of each wing. Using remaining wire, wrap around angel's neck and secure in back by wings. Trim wire. Wrap ¾"-wide gold ribbon around angel's neck. Tie bow in back of angel to cover wire and wing ends. Shape ribbon ends and cascade downward. Hot-glue greenery and flowers to angel body and top of angel head as desired. Tie estaz through eye screw for hanger.

Potpourri Covered Egg

Pictured on page 34

Materials:
Bowl. Cording: ⅛"-wide, dk. green, 1⅓ yds. Egg: wooden, 2½". Glue: craft; hot glue gun and glue sticks. Greenery: dried roses (3); dried assortment. Ribbon: ⅝"-wide ombre, green, ¼ yd. Potpourri. Scissors: fabric.

Embellishing:
Refer to picture on page 34. Place potpourri in bowl. Using craft glue, apply glue to one half side of egg. Roll egg in potpourri. Repeat above steps with other half of egg. Let glue dry. Wind cording around egg. Using hot glue gun and glue stick, secure cording with small amount of hot glue. Using ribbon, make bow. Hot-glue bow and greenery to egg.

Winter Wonderland Egg

Pictured on page 34

Materials:
Acrylic paint: metallic lt. blue. Beads: seed, yellow (3); flowers, pink (3). Buttons: decorative, ceramic rabbit; birdhouse. Egg: porcelain, unglazed, front opening, 4". Flowers: small purple fern-like. Glue: hot glue gun and glue sticks. Greenery: fern-like, for trees. Matchstick. Paintbrushes. Scissors: craft. Spanish moss. Trim: ¼"-wide elan, gold, 3". Tweezers. Wire: 20-gauge, floral, 4". Wire cutters.

Painting:
Refer to General Instructions For Egg Painting on pages 7-10. Paint inside of egg using metallic lt. blue paint.

Embellishing:
Refer to picture on page 34. Using scissors, cut off red tip of matchstick. Using hot glue gun and glue stick, hot-glue greenery for trees to inside back of egg. Hot-glue moss inside bottom of egg raising it to the bottom of egg opening. Create a path by hot-gluing one end of trim to inside back of egg. Bring trim out to egg opening, expanding trim gradually. Secure by hot-gluing. Hot-glue matchstick to back of birdhouse button. Hot-glue birdhouse inside of egg. Hot-glue yellow seed beads to center of pink flower beads. Cut three lengths of wire varying between ¾"-1½". Hot-glue wires into base of pink flowers. Hot-glue purple flowers around base of birdhouse button, using tweezers if necessary. Hot-glue pink flowers inside of egg. Hot-glue rabbit button onto trim path.

Mosaic Seashell Egg

Pictured on page 34

Materials:
Acrylic paint: metallic gold. Aluminum foil. Beads 4mm: white, pearl string, 24". Cardboard: lightweight, 1¼"-diameter. Egg: wooden, 2½". Glue: craft; découpage. Knife: craft. Motif: paper cherub or angel, 1¼"-1½" diameter. Paintbrush. Seashells: brown/white scallop, 1¼"-diameter (5); assorted small (3 types such as rose petal, pearly venetians, silver turbos, or spindles). Scissors. Sparkle glaze.

Painting:
Refer to General Instructions For Egg Painting on pages 7-10. Prepare egg for painting.
Basecoat egg using metallic gold paint.

Embellishing:
Using craft knife, cut out motif. Refer to picture on page 34. Using découpage glue, attach motif slightly below center of egg. Apply two coats of découpage glue over motif. Using craft glue, glue pearls, rose petal shells, turbos, scallops, pearly venetians, and spindles onto egg, referring to side and back view diagrams below. Place cardboard on aluminum foil. Cover cardboard with craft glue. Arrange five scallop shells around cardboard circle, forming base for egg. Glue egg onto base with craft glue. Apply sparkle glaze over entire egg and base.

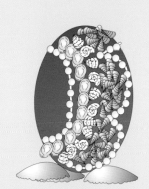 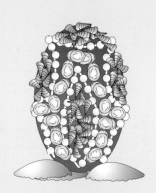

Side view   Back view

Frosting Egg

Pictured on page 34

Materials:
Decorating bag with tips: #3; #32; #104. Drying container. Egg: hard-boiled. Food coloring: red. Pan. Royal icing: recipe on page 92. Tea bags: black (3-4). Water. Wax paper.

Painting:
Refer to General Instructions Preparing Real Eggs on pages 9-10. Steep tea bags in one quart of water for several minutes. Place egg in tea and let egg soak until lt. tan (about five minutes). Let egg dry.

Embellishing:
Refer to picture on page 34. Tint frosting pink with couple of drops of red food coloring. Use tip #3 to apply icing lines and dots. Use tip #104 to create bow on top of egg. Use tip #32 to create petals on wax paper. Place egg into center of petals. Allow frosting to set up.

An Eggceptional Halloween

Ghost Egg

Pictured on page 36

Materials
Acrylic gesso. Acrylic paint: black; lt. blue; med. blue; white. Acrylic spray sealer. Cheese cloth. Craft foam: white. Egg: wooden, 4½". Glue: craft. Paintbrushes. Scissors.

Painting:
Refer to General Instructions For Egg Painting on pages 7-10. Prepare egg for painting. **Basecoat** egg using white paint. **Detail** egg referring to pattern. **Dot** eyes using white paint.

Embellishing:
Refer to Ghost Egg Pattern on page 90 and picture on page 36. Cut two arms from white craft foam. Cut cheese cloth circular and place over egg. Using craft glue, glue ends of cheese cloth to underneath side of egg and to top of egg. Glue arms to each side of egg.

Frankenstein Egg

Pictured on page 36

Materials
Acrylic gesso. Acrylic paint: black; lt. green/gray; orange; purple; white. Acrylic spray sealer. Drill with ⅜" bit. Egg: papier mâché, 5½". Glue: hot glue gun and glue sticks. Hacksaw. Napkin ring: wooden, for holder. Paintbrushes. Scissors: craft. Screws with bolts: ⅜" wide, 1½" long (2). Steel wool for hair.

Painting:
Using hacksaw, cut 1" off top of papier mâché egg. Using scissors, cut "cracks" in top edge of egg. Refer to General Instructions For Egg Painting on pages 7-10. Prepare egg for painting. **Basecoat** egg using lt. green/gray paint. **Detail** egg referring to pattern. Paint napkin ring holder using purple paint.

Embellishing:
Drill holes on both sides of jaw. Attach screws and bolts into drilled holes. Place egg on napkin ring holder. Insert steel wool into opening in head for hair.

Mummy Egg

Pictured on page 36

Materials
Acrylic gesso. Acrylic paint: black; lt. gray; med. gray; green; white. Acrylic spray sealer. Cheese cloth. Eggs: wooden, 1"; papier mâché, 4½". Glue: craft. Paintbrushes. Scissors.

Painting:
Refer to General Instructions For Egg Painting on pages 7-10. Prepare egg for painting. **Basecoat** eggs using lt. gray paint. Using craft glue, secure small egg onto large egg for nose. **Detail** egg referring to pattern. **Dot** eyes using white paint.

Embellishing:
Refer to picture on page 36. Cut and wrap 1"-wide strip of cheese cloth around egg. Glue beginning and ending of cheese cloth to secure.

Witch Egg

Pictured on page 36

Materials
Acrylic gesso. Acrylic paint: black; lavender; orange; metallic purple; metallic red; white; yellow. Acrylic spray sealer. Baking clay: white. Egg: papier mâché, 4". Glue: hot glue gun and glue sticks. Feathers: black-and-white boa, 6". Napkin ring: silver, for holder. Paintbrushes. Pen: fine-tip permanent, black. Stars: wooden, ½" (2); 1". Witch hat: 5", black felt.

Painting:
Refer to General Instructions For Egg Painting and Sculpting Baking Clay on pages 7-10. Sculpt clay into witch's nose. Bake clay following manufacturer's instructions. Hot-glue nose to egg. Prepare egg, clay, and wooden stars for painting. **Basecoat** egg and clay using lavender paint, 1" star using orange, one ½" star using yellow, and one ½" star using metallic purple paint. **Detail** egg referring to pattern.

Embellishing:
Refer to picture on page 36. Glue feathers around egg for hair. Distress hat by crumpling. Hot-glue hat in place. Hot-glue stars randomly onto hat. Hot-glue egg in napkin ring for holder.

Bat Egg

Pictured on page 35

Materials
Acrylic gesso. Acrylic paint: black; lavender; purple; white. Acrylic spray sealer. Craft foam: black. Egg: wooden, 2½". Glue: hot glue gun and glue sticks. Paintbrushes. Scissors. Toothpicks.

Painting:
Refer to General Instructions For Egg Painting on pages 7-10. Prepare egg for painting. Refer to Bat Egg Patterns on page 89. Cut two wings and two ears from craft foam. **Basecoat** egg wings, and ears using purple paint. **Detail** egg and wings referring to pattern. Use toothpick for small details. Using hot glue gun and glue stick, hot-glue wings to egg sides bending them in center for curved effect. Hot-glue ears to egg.

Pumpkin Egg

Pictured on page 35

Materials
Acrylic gesso. Acrylic paint: black; dk. green; lt. green; orange; dk. orange. Acrylic spray sealer. Egg: wooden, 2½". Paintbrushes.

Painting:
Refer to General Instructions For Egg Painting on pages 7-10. Prepare egg for painting. **Basecoat** egg using orange paint. **Detail** egg referring to pattern.

Spider Egg

Pictured on page 35

Materials
Acrylic gesso. Acrylic paint: black; gray; purple; white. Acrylic spray sealer. Chenille stems: 6" long, black (8). Egg: wooden, 2½". Glue: hot glue gun and glue sticks. Paintbrushes.

Painting:
Refer to General Instructions For Egg Painting on pages 7-10. Prepare egg for painting. **Basecoat** egg using black paint. **Detail** egg referring to pattern. **Dot** eyes using white, black, then white paint again. **Dot** body using purple paint.

Embellishing:
For spider legs, bend one chenille stem in half. Bend again at 30° angle 2½" from first bend. Bend end of chenille stem for feet. Repeat for total of eight legs. Twist ends of four legs together. Refer to picture on page 35. Using hot glue gun and glue stick, hot-glue legs to each side of egg.

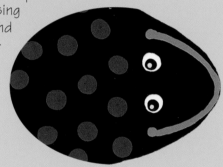

Dracula Egg

Pictured on page 35

Materials
Acrylic gesso. Acrylic paint: black; flesh; pink; white. Acrylic spray sealer. Cotton swabs. Craft foam: black; white. Egg: wooden, 2½". Glue: hot glue gun and glue sticks. Paintbrushes. Scissors.

Painting:
Refer to General Instructions For Egg Painting on pages 7-10. Prepare egg for painting. **Basecoat** egg using flesh paint. **Detail** egg referring to pattern. **Dot** eyes using white then black paint. Using cotton swab, lightly dab pink paint for rosy cheeks.

Embellishing:
Refer to Dracula Egg Patterns on page 89. Cut cape from black craft foam and collar from white craft foam. Using hot glue gun and glue stick, hot-glue collar onto egg. Hot-glue cape at base of egg, turning back cape ends.

Trick or Treat Egg

Pictured on page 35

Materials

Acrylic gesso. Acrylic paint: orange; white; yellow. Acrylic spray sealer. Egg: wooden, 2½". Paintbrushes. Pen: fine-point permanent, black. Pencil.

Painting:

Refer to General Instructions For Egg Painting on pages 7-10. Prepare egg for painting. Mark egg into three sections using pencil referring to pattern. **Basecoat** top section using white, middle section using orange, and lower section using yellow paint. **Detail** lettering using pen.

Owl Egg

Pictured on page 35

Materials:

Acrylic gesso. Acrylic paint: black; copper; gray; orange; tan; dk. tan; white; off-white; yellow. Acrylic spray sealer. Branch: 1" x 12". Drill with ⅛" bit. Egg: wooden, 4½". Glue: craft. Paintbrushes. Wire: picture hanging, 1 yd. Wire cutters.

Painting:

Refer to General Instructions For Egg Painting on pages 7-10. Prepare egg for painting. Drill two holes in bottom of egg for feet. **Basecoat** egg using off-white paint. **Detail** egg referring to pattern. **Float** dk. tan paint around wings, tail, and under beak.

Embellishing:

Cut two 8½" lengths of wire. Twist wire into feet shape. Paint feet using copper paint. Using craft glue, secure feet into holes on bottom of egg. Place owl on branch.

Stacked Pumpkin Eggs

Pictured on page 35

Materials

Acrylic gesso. Acrylic paint: black; med. brown; gold; lt. gold; red; off-white. Acrylic spray sealer. Bell: ½" diameter, gold. Dowels: ⅛" x 1½"; ⁵⁄₁₆" x 1½". Drill with ⅛" and ⁵⁄₁₆" bits. Eggs: wooden, 4½"; 3½"; 2½". Fabric: cotton plaid, ¼ yd. or purchase hat; 1½"-wide wool, 12". Glue: hot glue gun and glue sticks; wood. Needle: hand-sewing. Paintbrushes. Pen: fine-tip permanent, black. Thread: coordinating. Twigs: (2).

Painting:

Refer to General Instructions For Egg Painting on pages 7-10. Drill ⁵⁄₁₆" hole in top of largest egg and bottom of middle egg. Drill ⅛" hole in top of middle egg and bottom of small egg. Drill holes in each side of middle egg to accommodate diameter of twigs. Prepare eggs for painting. **Basecoat** eggs using lt. gold paint. **Detail** eggs referring to pattern. **Float** rib lines on eggs using med. brown paint.

Embellishing:

Using wood gel, glue twigs into middle body section. Glue body sections together using dowels. Make or purchase hat. Sew bell on tip of hat. Hot-glue hat on top of pumpkin head. Fray ends of wool fabric for scarf. Tie scarf around pumpkin's neck.

Duck Egg

Pictured on page 35

Materials:

Acrylic gesso. Acrylic paint: black; dk. gray; lt. gray; metallic green; dk. orange; dk. tan; lt. tan; white; yellow. Acrylic spray sealer. Craft foam: brown; yellow. Dowel: wooden, ⅜" x 6". Drill with ⅜" bit. Eggs: wooden, 4½"; 2½". Feathers: small, speckled brown. Glue: hot glue gun and glue sticks. Knife: craft. Paintbrushes. Sandpaper. Scissors: craft. Wheel: wooden, 1" for neck. Wood: ¼" baltic birch, 4" x 4".

Painting:

Refer to General Instructions for Egg Painting on pages 7-10. Sand flat bottom of eggs to round off. Drill holes in both eggs for neck, legs, and tail. Sand any rough edges. Refer to Duck Egg Patterns on page 89. Cut two feet from baltic birch. Cut three 2" lengths from dowel. Prepare egg and all wood pieces for painting. **Basecoat** small egg using metallic green paint.

Detail eggs, dowels, feet, neck, and wooden wheel referring to pattern. **Float** around edge and along middle of chest using dk. gray paint. **Float** around edges of wing area using dk. tan paint. **Dot** eyes using white, black, then white paint.

Embellishing:

Cut two wings from brown craft foam and one upper and lower beak from yellow craft foam. Using hot glue gun and glue stick, hot-glue head on dowel and push through wheel into body. Hot-glue dowels onto feet then into duck's body. Hot-glue wings and beak onto egg. Hot-glue feathers onto egg for tail.

Wire Crow Egg

Pictured on page 35

Materials:

Acrylic gesso. Acrylic paint: dk. blue; bright gold; fuchsia. Acrylic spray sealer. Egg: wooden, 2½". Drill with bit width of wire. Glue: wood. Paintbrushes. Pliers. Wire: 18-gauge, bailing, 28". Wire cutters.

Painting:

Refer to General Instructions For Egg Painting on pages 7-10. Drill two holes in lower part of egg for legs. Prepare egg for painting. **Basecoat** egg using dk. blue paint. **Detail** egg referring to

pattern. **Comma stroke** side of eyes using bright gold paint.

Embellishing:

Using wire cutters, cut wire desired length for legs and feet. Using pliers, bend wire for legs and feet. Using wood glue, glue legs into drilled holes in lower part of egg.

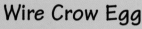

Chick-in Egg

Pictured on page 35

Materials:

Acrylic gesso. Acrylic paint: black; med. brown; flesh; orange; white; yellow. Acrylic spray sealer. Egg: wooden, 2½". Paintbrushes. Toothbrush.

Painting:

Refer to General Instructions For Egg Painting

on pages 7-10. Prepare egg for painting. **Basecoat** top section of egg using yellow and bottom section of egg using flesh paint. **Detail** egg referring to pattern. **Splatter** egg using med. brown paint.

Eggspecially For You

Whale Egg

Pictured on page 39

Materials:
Acrylic gesso. Acrylic paint: black; cream; gray; gray/green; lt. blue; white. Acrylic spray sealer. Bead spray: iridescent. Drill with ⁵⁄₁₆" bit. Craft foam: gray; white. Glue: craft. Paintbrushes. Sandpaper. Sponge.

Painting:
Refer to General Instructions for Egg Painting on pages 7-10. Sand flat bottom of egg to round off. Prepare egg for painting. **Basecoat** egg using lt. blue paint. **Detail** egg referring to pattern. **Sponge** back of whale using gray paint. **Float** under eyes and top of mouth using gray paint. **Detail** mouth using cream paint. Using fan brush, **detail** mouth first using gray, then gray/green paint. **Dot** eyes using black then white paint.

Embellishing:
Refer to Whale Egg Patterns on page 92. Cut out one tail from each color of craft foam. Cut out two fins from each color of craft foam. Using craft glue, glue gray foam pieces to white foam pieces. Glue tail and fins to egg. Drill ⁵⁄₁₆" hole in top of egg for water spout. Glue bead spray into drilled hole for water spout.

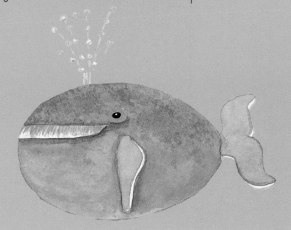

Polar Bear Egg

Pictured on page 39

Materials:
Acrylic gesso. Acrylic paint: black; gray; pink; white. Acrylic spray sealer. Egg: wooden, 4½". Paintbrushes. Sandpaper.

Painting:
Refer to General Instructions For Egg Painting on pages 7-10. Sand flat bottom of egg to round off. Prepare egg for painting. **Basecoat** egg using white paint. **Detail** face on narrow part of egg and tail on wide part of egg referring to pattern.

Panda Egg

Pictured on page 39

Materials:
Acrylic gesso. Acrylic paint: black; gray; pink; white. Acrylic spray sealer. Egg: wooden, 4½". Paintbrushes. Sandpaper.

Painting:
Refer to General Instructions For Egg Painting on pages 7-10. Prepare egg for painting. Sand flat bottom of egg to round off. **Basecoat** egg using white paint. **Detail** egg referring to pattern.

Penguin Eggs

Pictured on page 39

Materials:
Acrylic gesso. Acrylic paint: black; dk. gray/blue; red; white; dk. yellow. Acrylic spray sealer. Craft foam: yellow. Eggs: wooden, 2½" (2). Glitter: iridescent. Glue: craft; spray. Paintbrushes. Marker pen: orange.

Painting:
Refer to General Instructions For Egg Painting on pages 7-10. Prepare eggs for painting. **Basecoat** eggs using white paint. **Detail** eggs referring to pattern.

Embellishing:
Refer to Penguin Eggs Pattern on page 91 and picture on page 39. Cut out two feet from craft foam for each penguin. Using orange marker pen, shade feet. Using craft glue, secure feet to bottom of egg. Using spray glue, spray top and back of eggs lightly and sprinkle glitter over glue.

Spaceman Egg

Pictured on page 40

Materials:
Acrylic gesso. Acrylic paint: black; blue; dk. blue; flesh; gray; green; pink; red; white; yellow. Acrylic spray sealer. Egg: wooden, 2½". Glue: craft. Half eggs: wooden, ⅞", (2). Paintbrushes. Sparkle glaze. Spools: wooden, ½" x ½" (2). Star: wooden, 3".

Painting:
Refer to General Instructions For Egg Painting on pages 7-10. Prepare eggs, spools, and star for painting. **Basecoat** eggs and spools using white paint. **Basecoat** star using dk. blue paint.

Detail eggs, spools, and star referring to pattern. Apply sparkle glaze on star.

Embellishing:
Using craft glue, secure spools to bottom of egg for legs. Glue half eggs to bottom of spools for feet. Glue feet to star.

Spaceship Egg

Pictured on page 40

Materials:
Acrylic gesso. Acrylic paint: dk. blue; metallic silver. Acrylic spray sealer. Button: 1¼" round with wire loop on top. Craft foam: blue. Drill with bit diameter of wire. Egg: wooden, 4½". Glue: craft; super. Paintbrush. Pencil. Scissors: craft. Stickers: star (3). Tinsel: wire stars. Wire: 18" x ⅟₃₂".

Painting:
Refer to General Instructions For Egg Painting on pages 7-10. Drill two holes in bottom of egg. Using super glue, secure button to flat portion of egg. Prepare egg for painting. **Basecoat** egg using metallic silver paint. **Detail** egg referring to pattern. **Float** along "seams" of spaceship and under ladder rungs using dk. blue paint.

Embellishing:
Fold craft foam in half. Using craft glue, secure craft foam halves together to layer. Refer to Spaceship Egg Pattern on page 91. Cut three fins from foam. Using super glue, secure fins to space ship. Wind wire around pencil tightly at bottom, loose at top. Hook wire end into button loop. Glue star tinsel between fins. Attach star stickers to fins.

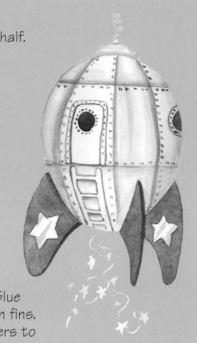

Airplane Egg

Pictured on page 40

Materials:
Acrylic gesso. Acrylic paint: black; gray; silver; white. Acrylic spray sealer. Button: wooden, 1⅛". Craft foam: gray; red. Eggs: wooden, 4½"; ⅞" (4). Fabric marker: black. Glue: craft. Paintbrushes. Ribbon: adhesive, red. Scissors: craft. Stickers: metallic star (2).

Painting:
Refer to General Instructions For Egg Painting on pages 7-10. Prepare eggs for painting. Basecoat top half of 4½" egg using white and bottom half of egg using silver paint. Basecoat ⅞" eggs using silver paint. Detail eggs referring to pattern.

Embellishing:
Place adhesive ribbon between white and silver paint. Draw circles on adhesive ribbon with fabric marker for windows. Using craft scissors, cut gray and red craft foam sheets in half. Using craft glue, secure gray and red craft foam pieces together. Refer to Airplane Egg Patterns on page 89. Cut two large wings and two small wings from gray craft foam. Cut one tail from red craft foam. Glue two small painted eggs on underside of each large wing for engines. Glue wings and tail to egg. Attach metallic stars on tail.

Dragon Eggs

Note: All dragons are made in same manner. White clay may be used then painted. Materials and instructions are for the flying dragon. Other dragons are optional ideas.

Pictured on page 37

Materials:
Acrylic gesso. Acrylic paint: dk. green; lt. green; pink; orange; yellow. Baking clay: burgundy; green; orange; pink; white; yellow. Drill with bit diameter of eye screw. Eye screw: small. Knife: craft. Egg: wooden, 2½". Glue: craft. Fishing line: 24". Paintbrush. Pencil. Toothpicks.

Painting:
Refer to General Instructions For Egg Painting and Sculpting Baking Clay on pages 7-10. Drill one hole in top of egg for eye screw. Prepare eggs for painting. **Basecoat** and **detail** egg, referring to pattern.

Embellishing:
Using green clay, shape clay in egg shape 1½" long for head. Using craft knife, cut slot for mouth. Pull top up and forward. Make indentations across top of nose with craft knife. Using orange clay, roll two small balls for eyes. Make two eye holes in head with pencil and push eyes in holes. Punch holes in center of eyes with toothpick. Using green clay, roll four thin green pieces ⅛" thick. Place one over each eye for eyebrows. Place remaining two for nostrils. Using green clay, shape ears. Using pink clay, make thin pink layer for inside ear. Bend ears into shape and place on head. Using orange and yellow clay for horns, roll each color ⅛" thick. Twist together so stripes go around. Cut two horns ¾" long. Make horns pointed at one end. Place horns between ears. Using pink clay, roll ¾" long piece, flatten and place in mouth for tongue. Using one-fourth yellow and three-fourths green, roll strip 3" long and ¾" thick (½ for neck, ½ for tail). Using craft knife, cut roll into sections, making each section smaller. Flatten each section with thumb and place one on top of another from largest to smallest. Narrow end of neck attaches to head, wide end of tail attaches to body. Using green clay, form front and back legs. Using yellow clay, make wings referring to Flying Pig Egg Diagram on page 90. Using burgundy clay, make triangle shapes for back spines and for end of tail. Shape all clay pieces to form to egg. Carefully remove and bake, following manufacturer's instructions. Using craft glue, secure clay pieces to egg. Attach eye screw into drilled hole in egg. Loop fishing line through eye screw and tie knot to secure.

Ostrich Celestial Egg

Pictured on page 41

Materials:
Acrylic gesso. Acrylic paint: dk. blue; blue/green; metallic gold; maroon. Acrylic spray sealer. Egg: ostrich. Glue: rubber cement. Paintbrush. Pencil. Scissors: craft. Sponge. Tracing paper.

Painting:
Refer to General Instructions For Painting Eggs on pages 7-10. Prepare egg for painting.
Basecoat egg using metallic gold paint. Refer to Ostrich Celestial Egg Patterns on page 91. Cut out four stars and one moon from tracing paper. Coat one side of moon pattern with rubber cement. Let rubber cement dry until tacky. Refer to picture on page 41. Press moon pattern onto upper half of one side of egg. Smooth pattern in place with fingers. Repeat to glue one star pattern just beyond and between points of moon. Glue remaining stars around egg, placing randomly. **Sponge** egg sparingly, just to edges of each pattern, using dk. blue paint allowing gold paint to show through. *Note: Do not sponge over patterns.* **Sponge** sides of egg using maroon and blue/green paint. Carefully peel off glued patterns. Touch up edges of gold stars and moon if needed.

Ostrich Lace Egg

Pictured on page 41

Materials:

Blow dryer. Cotton balls. Dremel tool with sanding disc. Egg: ostrich. Fabric paint: pearl. Graphite paper. Nightlight fixture with cord and switch. Pencil. Towel. Tracing paper. Window cleaner.

Painting:

Refer to picture on page 41. Place egg on large folded towel. Using dremel tool with sanding disc on low speed, enlarge hole in bottom of egg to 1¼" wide. Check fit of nightlight fixture and adjust hole size if necessary. Refer to Ostrich Lace Egg Patterns on page 91. Trace flower patterns onto small pieces of tracing paper. Randomly transfer flower patterns to egg using graphite paper. Add leaves as desired to obtain flowing pattern. Following patterns, squeeze out thin lines of fabric paint to complete flowers. After each flower is painted, dry with blow dryer to avoid smearing. Allow egg to dry thoroughly for approximately twelve hours. Clean graphite lines from egg using cotton balls and window cleaner. Rub very gently to avoid removing paint. Rinse with water and pat dry.

Embellishing:

Attach nightlight fixture inside egg.

Gargoyle Eggs

Pictured on page 38

Materials:

Acrylic gesso. Acrylic paint: black; gray. Baking clay: white. Eggs: wooden, 2½"; 1¾". Glue: hot glue gun and glue sticks. Knife: craft. Paint: granite stone texture. Paintbrushes. Pencil. Toothpicks.

Painting:

Refer to General Instructions For Egg Painting and Sculpting Baking Clay on pages 7-10. Sculpt each wing from 1" ball of clay. Flatten clay. Using pencil, form three to four indentations along one edge of clay. Flatten clay again. Form clay to egg body. Roll clay rope 4" x ½". Twist to make wrinkles. Flatten one end of clay for foot. Using craft knife, make two cuts in clay foot for toes. Pinch clay to form points. Form legs to egg. Roll clay ropes 2" x ⅓", form arms same as legs. Shape ears from triangular shapes. Shape horns. Form ears and horns to head egg. Shape ¼" balls for eyes. Roll small strips, lay over tops of eyes and form to egg. Cut ¼" off both ends of ten toothpicks for spikes. Make collar by flattening a 1" ball of clay. Form between head and body. Push toothpick spikes into collar. Bake clay, following manufacturer's instructions. Using hot glue gun and glue stick, hot-glue clay pieces to egg. Prepare eggs for painting.

Basecoat egg using gray paint. Apply granite stone texture over gray paint. This may take multiple coats to reach desired effect. **Detail** gargoyles referring to pattern.

Patterns

Airplane Egg Patterns
Page 85 • Enlarge 200%

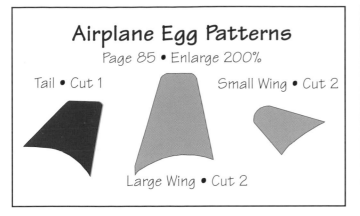

Tail • Cut 1

Small Wing • Cut 2

Large Wing • Cut 2

Button Leg Chick Egg Patterns
Page 49 • Enlarge 165%

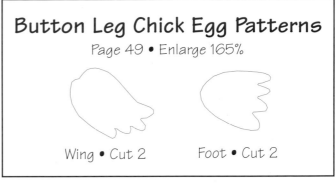

Wing • Cut 2

Foot • Cut 2

Bat Egg Patterns
Page 79 • Enlarge 250%

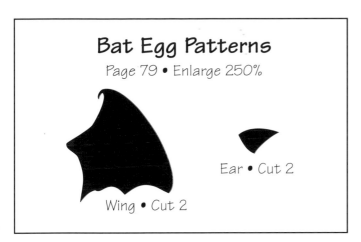

Ear • Cut 2

Wing • Cut 2

Dracula Egg Patterns
Page 80 • Enlarge 190%

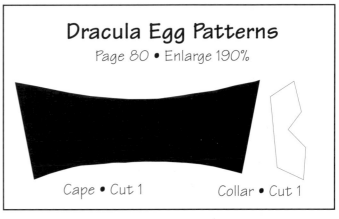

Cape • Cut 1

Collar • Cut 1

Bunny Wagon Eggs Pattern
Page 47 • Enlarge 250%

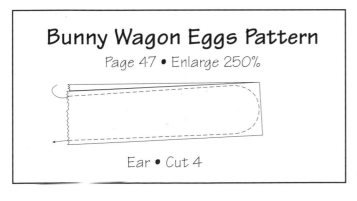

Ear • Cut 4

Duck Egg Patterns
Page 82 • Enlarge 185%

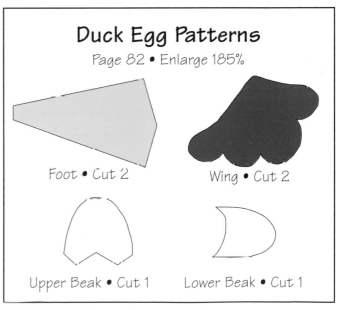

Foot • Cut 2

Wing • Cut 2

Upper Beak • Cut 1

Lower Beak • Cut 1

Butterfly Egg Patterns
Page 48 • Enlarge 165%

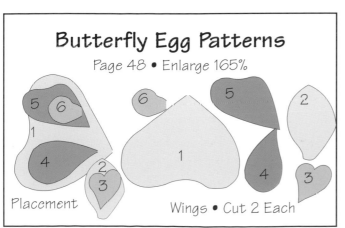

Placement

Wings • Cut 2 Each

Patterns

Egg in Disguise Patterns
Page 47 • Enlarge 350%

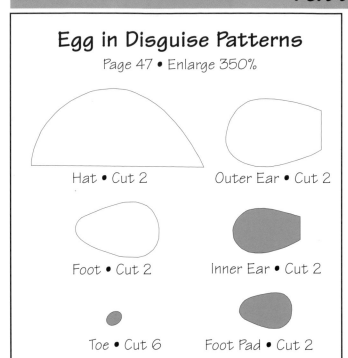

Hat • Cut 2

Outer Ear • Cut 2

Foot • Cut 2

Inner Ear • Cut 2

Toe • Cut 6

Foot Pad • Cut 2

Hatched Egg Patterns
Page 51 • Enlarge 165%

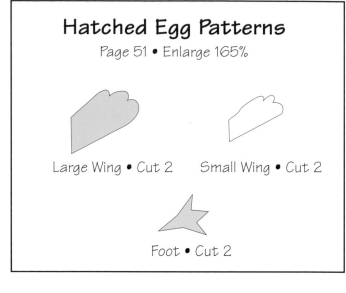

Large Wing • Cut 2

Small Wing • Cut 2

Foot • Cut 2

Kittens & Mittens Egg Trio Pattern
Page 52 • Enlarge 315%

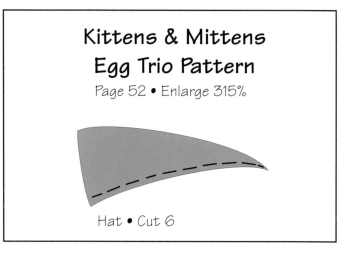

Hat • Cut 6

Flying Pig Egg Diagram
Page 50

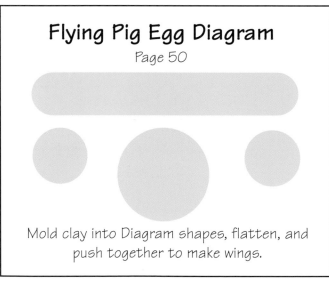

Mold clay into Diagram shapes, flatten, and push together to make wings.

Lamb Egg Patterns
Page 51 • Full Size

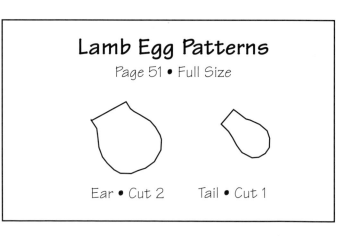

Ear • Cut 2

Tail • Cut 1

Ghost Egg Pattern
Page 78 • Enlarge 180%

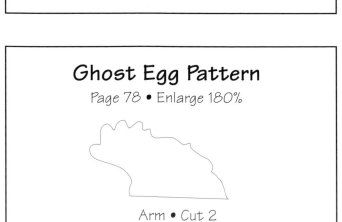

Arm • Cut 2

Patterns

Ostrich Celestial Egg Patterns
Page 87 • Enlarge 240%

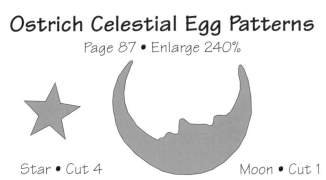

Star • Cut 4   Moon • Cut 1

Ostrich Lace Egg Patterns
Page 88 • Enlarge 225%

Penguin Eggs Pattern
Page 84 • Full Size

Foot • Cut 4

Rabbits in a Shoe Eggs Patterns
Page 53 • Enlarge 260%

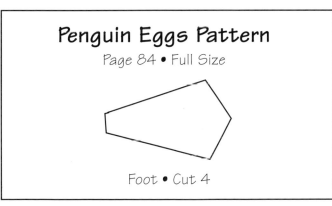

Small Ear • Cut 6   Large Ear • Cut 2

Rooster Egg Patterns
Page 52 • Enlarge 280%

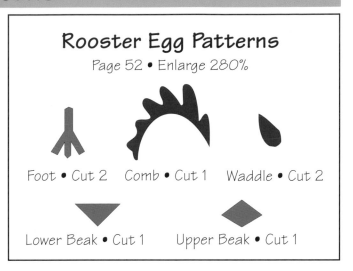

Foot • Cut 2   Comb • Cut 1   Waddle • Cut 2

Lower Beak • Cut 1   Upper Beak • Cut 1

Rudolph Egg Patterns
Page 74 • Enlarge 230%

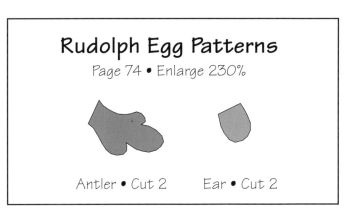

Antler • Cut 2   Ear • Cut 2

Spaceship Egg Pattern
Page 85 • Enlarge 320%

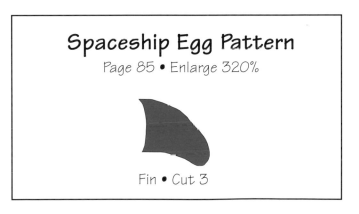

Fin • Cut 3

Stenciled Tree Egg Patterns
Page 60 • Enlarge 200%

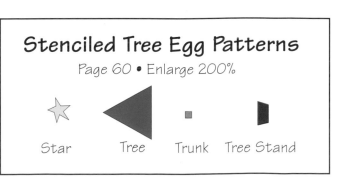

Star   Tree   Trunk   Tree Stand

Patterns

Sunflower Egg Patterns
Page 49 • Enlarge 250%

Sunflower • Cut 1   Leaves • Cut 2

Whale Egg Patterns
Page 83 • Enlarge 190%

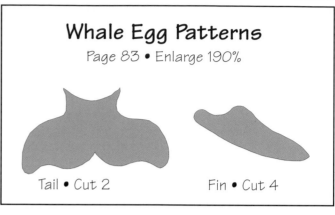

Tail • Cut 2   Fin • Cut 4

Teddy Bear Egg Patterns
Page 71 • Enlarge 260%

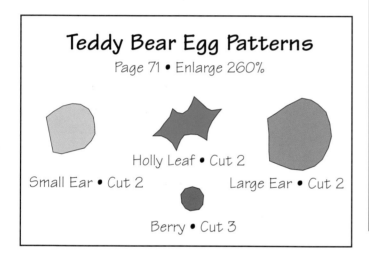

Holly Leaf • Cut 2

Small Ear • Cut 2   Large Ear • Cut 2

Berry • Cut 3

Paper Reindeer Egg Patterns
Page 72 • Enlarge 210%

Reindeer Head   Nose

Tissue Paper Tree Egg Patterns
Page 71 • Enlarge 230%

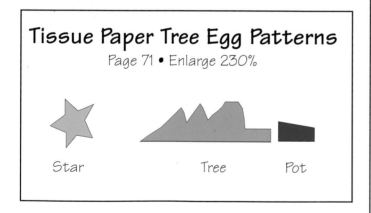

Star   Tree   Pot

Royal Icing
Page 78

1 box (1 lb.) confectioners' sugar
2 Tbs. powdered egg whites
6 Tbs. water
⅛ tsp. cream of tartar
Food coloring

In large bowl, using electric mixer on low, mix confectioners' sugar, egg white powder, water, and cream of tartar until combined. Increase speed to high and continue beating until stiff peaks form.

If not using icing immediately, place a piece of plastic wrap directly on surface of icing and store in refrigerator for up to one week. Bring to room temperature before using.

To tint icing transfer icing to bowl(s). Tint desired color using food coloring.

Ribbon Diagrams

5-Petal Flower

Beginning ¼" from edge, trace five 1½" half circles on ribbon. Trim ribbon ¼" past last half circle.

Gather stitch on traced half circles with continuous gather stitch. See (1).

Pull gather and secure thread. See (2).

Join last petal to first petal for completed 5-petal flower. See (3).

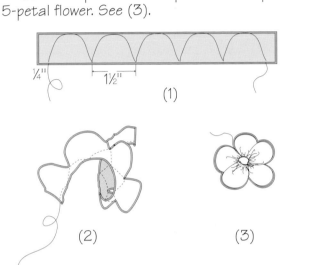

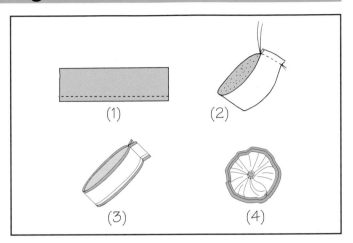

Gathered Flower, Single-Ribbon

Cut ribbon into 5" length. Fold and sew short ends together. See (1). Secure thread.

Gather-stitch along one edge lengthwise. See (2).

Pull gather tightly and secure thread for completed single-ribbon gathered flower. See (3).

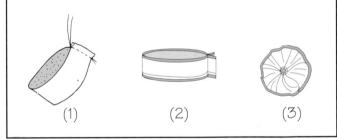

Fan

Accordion fold 5" wired ribbon. See (1).

Fan ribbon and tack for completed fan. See (2).

Poppy

Fold 9" length of ribbon in half lengthwise. Gather-stitch along raw edges. See (1).

Pull gather and secure thread. See (2). Tack bottom edge in a spiral manner for completed poppy. See (3).

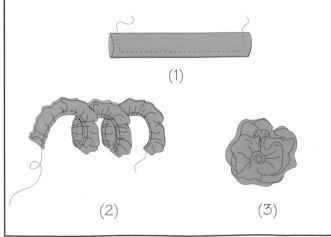

Gathered Flower, Double-Ribbon

See diagrams top of next column. Cut ribbon into two 5" lengths. Lay one 5" piece on top of other 5" piece. Sew together along one edge lengthwise. See (1).

Fold and sew short ends together. See (2). Secure thread.

Gather-stitch along one edge lengthwise. See (3).

Pull gather tightly and secure thread for completed double-ribbon gathered flower. See (4).

Index

Metric Equivalency Chart

mm-millimetres   cm-centimetres
inches to millimetres and centimetres

inches	mm	cm	inches	cm	inches	cm
⅛	3	0.3	9	22.9	30	76.2
¼	6	0.6	10	25.4	31	78.7
½	13	1.3	12	30.5	33	83.8
⅝	16	1.6	13	33.0	34	86.4
¾	19	1.9	14	35.6	35	88.9
⅞	22	2.2	15	38.1	36	91.4
1	25	2.5	16	40.6	37	94.0
1¼	32	3.2	17	43.2	38	96.5
1½	38	3.8	18	45.7	39	99.1
1¾	44	4.4	19	48.3	40	101.6
2	51	5.1	20	50.8	41	104.1
2½	64	6.4	21	53.3	42	106.7
3	76	7.6	22	55.9	43	109.2
3½	89	8.9	23	58.4	44	111.8
4	102	10.2	24	61.0	45	114.3
4½	114	11.4	25	63.5	46	116.8
5	127	12.7	26	66.0	47	119.4
6	152	15.2	27	68.6	48	121.9
7	178	17.8	28	71.1	49	124.5
8	203	20.3	29	73.7	50	127.0